Picture Framing

Anne and Jane Cope
Picture Framing

photography by John Warren
line drawings by Jane Cope

Pan Original
Pan Books London and Sydney

First published 1981 by Pan Books Ltd,
Cavaye Place, London SW10 9PG
© Anne and Jane Cope 1981
ISBN 0 330 26346 3
Printed and bound in Great Britain by
Morrison & Gibb Ltd, London and Edinburgh

Contents

Acknowledgements

Our thanks go to the following artists for loaning their work to be framed – Lorna Arnott (acrylic paintings, page **62** and page **70**), Morris Nitsun (oil paintings, page **69** and page **70**), Mary Bridger (etching, page **58**), Livia Edelstein (satin ribbon weave, page **72**), Sally Geeve (needlepoint sampler, page **71**) and Tracy Jackling (poster painting, page **70**); also to Clare Osborne ('Trout' by Martin Knowlden, page **34**) and Malcolm Smith (medals, page **71**) who kindly lent us subjects for framing.

For permission to reproduce the other subjects framed in this book we would like to thank, The National Gallery (Edward VI, page **71**), The National Portrait Gallery ('A Woman', page **71**), The National Maritime Museum ('Celestial Planisphere of the Northern and Southern Hemispheres', page **36**), Publications Department, Kew Gardens (botanical illustrations, page **72**), London Transport (photograph, page **72**), Galerie Welz, Salzburg (Egon Schiele self-portrait, page **46**), and Private Eye Publications (Hector Breeze cartoon, page **47**).

Introduction

Every picture is a unique combination of shapes, lines and colours. The framer's job is to create a setting in which they will be seen to best advantage. It would be quite wrong to say that it is the frame which makes the picture, but in a sense a picture does not fully exist until it has a frame, and it is the business of completing this creative process which gives the greatest satisfaction.

A common reaction we met with while writing this book was that although most people know more or less what framing involves and feel fairly confident about putting a frame together, they are less certain about choosing appropriate frame styles, colours and proportions. This is where we have particularly tried to help, not that matters of taste can be reduced to sets of rules. As with any craft a satisfactory end product often turns out to be a mixture of convention, imagination and common sense.

This book is aimed at the amateur but in the course of it we have covered most of the techniques a professional framer is likely to encounter in an average month's work, plus a few more. If you read the first two chapters you will be in possession of the essentials of framing. The rest of the book is devoted to various pictorial genres and to the frames which suit them best, and also to more unusual frames and frame finishes.

Picture framing is one of the most accessible and satisfying of spare-time occupations. Materials and equipment can be bought from any reasonably stocked art shop or tool shop and they are not, by comparison with those of some other crafts, particularly expensive. Almost everyone has something they would like framed. Prove to them that you can make respectable mitred corners and the job is yours!

Anne and Jane Cope

CHAPTER I

Materials and equipment

Components of a frame

In all likelihood you are well acquainted with how a traditional picture frame is assembled, but just in case you're a bit hazy have a look at **Fig. 1a**.

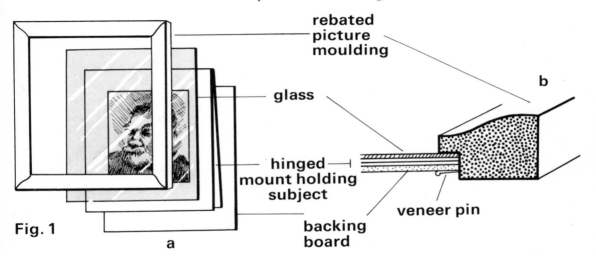

rebated
picture
moulding

glass

b

hinged
mount holding
subject

veneer pin

Fig. 1

backing
board

a

Mouldings

Fig. 2

front/face sight
edge

back

rebate

bottom

The essential prerequisite for picture framing and one that will exercise your discrimination most is the picture moulding, so a word about this first. **Fig. 1b** and **Fig. 2** show cross-sections of a piece of picture moulding and define some of the terms we use later on. The rebate or 'rabbet' is the recess which holds the glass, mount, picture and back board. These days, picture mouldings in various sorts of wood are expertly sawn and milled to produce a fascinating variety of profiles with beads and bevels, flutes, scoops and lips. Add to this a further variation introduced by staining, colouring and gilding and you have a veritable plethora of mouldings to choose from. The photograph on page **33** illustrates just a selection of the innumerable types available. So, where do you buy these ready-finished mouldings?

It's a little difficult to give a helpful list of suppliers because a very varied range of moulding is available from such a large number of places. The best advice is to look in your Yellow Pages under 'Picture Framers', 'Artists' Materials' and 'Do-it-yourself Shops' and ring around to find out who stocks what.

You might think the obvious source would be an established picture framer who of course is bound to keep a good selection of moulding in stock. But in our experience their usual answer to a request for a length of moulding is 'no', they won't sell you a length you can cut up yourself but they will cut you some mitred lengths that you can put together yourself. Quite simply they make their money by selling their expertise, not the materials of the trade. Nevertheless, ask your local framer if he's willing to sell by the length. You may be lucky and find he looks kindly on amateurs.

The best bet for mouldings is an art shop that also runs a picture-framing business. Selling a tube of paint or a length of picture moulding is all one to them. A 'length' may be anything from 6 to 9 ft; it varies from moulding to moulding, and is priced per foot. Quoting prices is risky in these inflationary times, but just to give you an idea, at the time of writing they ranged from about 50p per foot to £2 and over. That is, 50p for a thin, plain wood moulding to just over £1 for something more complicated and upwards of £1.75 for very heavy ornate types. Many very fine mouldings are imported from the Continent, especially Italy, and are consequently more expensive than the 'home-grown' ones.

Should you want to buy just a few feet rather than a whole length, many shops will oblige but charge a percentage extra. Like full-time picture framers they will also cut you mitred lengths and charge a small amount for the cuts. If you decide to have mitred lengths cut, remember that most framers work to the 'rebate size'. That means the overall size of the subject to be framed, so just give him those dimensions.

The third source for picture moulding is a DIY shop or perhaps a timber yard. These frequently stock a limited

Fig. 3

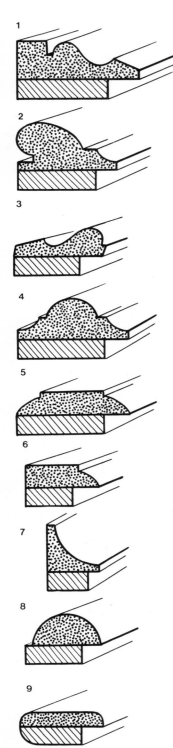

range of plain pine or ramin (a light-coloured hardwood) mouldings, sold by the length.

Now a couple of points to bear in mind when you are buying. The length you require has to take account of the width of the moulding. A simple equation for computing how much you need is given on page **28**. Secondly, steer clear of solid metal mouldings. They cannot be cut or joined satisfactorily by the tools we suggest. On the other hand there are 'metal look' mouldings which consist of a wooden moulding faced with a thin metal skin. These can be cut perfectly well with mitre-box and tenon-saw and are joined just like normal wooden mouldings.

Making your own picture mouldings

Sometimes you can't find quite what you want amongst the ready-finished mouldings, or the one you do fancy is a bit costly. Making up your own picture moulding can solve both problems.

Timber yards and some DIY merchants keep stocks of moulded pine lengths made for use as architraves, chair or picture rails, and cover moulding etc. (Ramin is available too but usually in plainer sections.) Naturally these mouldings don't have a rebate so you simply glue on a plain oblong or square length to make one. In fact if you look at some of the more complex ready-finished mouldings you will see that many consist of several sections glued together. **Fig. 3** shows some of the possibilities – the crosshatched parts represent the added rebate. No. **1** is the type used for the black frame on page **71** and the pine frame on page **35**; No. **7** the sort used for the red frame on page **71** and the frame with the dark mount on page **35**. No. **3** was used to make the frame on page **69**. Note that the rebate in No. **8** adds a lip to an otherwise plain moulding, and that a shaped rebate length is used in No. **9** to lend interest to the side of the moulding. When you buy the wood, check for bad knots or splits and look along the length to make sure it isn't bowed or warped.

How do you glue the sections together? Well, first of all cut the wood into pieces a little longer than your mitred lengths need to be, avoiding knots and extra-rough patches. Glue the sections together using Evo-stik Woodworking Adhesive and wipe off excess glue with a damp cloth. If there

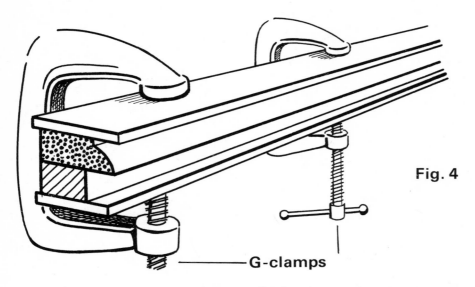

Fig. 4

G-clamps

are two flat bearing surfaces, clamp the sections between a couple of pieces of spare wood using G-clamps **(Fig. 4)**. If you are short on clamps or your sections are a difficult shape, hold them together with thick elastic bands. These need to be wound tightly round in several places, and to prevent the rebate section from sliding out of position under pressure from the bands, tap in a few veneer pins **(Fig. 5)**.

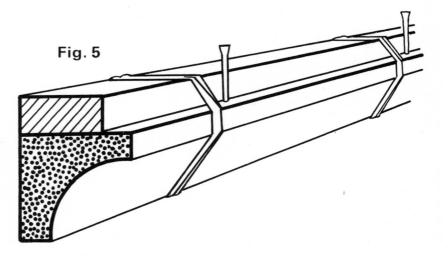

Fig. 5

Alternatively, hold the sections together with masking tape wrapped tightly around.

When everything is firmly stuck, sand the completed moulding well, finishing off with flour paper. See Chapter 8 for hints on waxing, staining and painting.

Tools for cutting and joining

Mitre-box To help you cut the 45° corner angles you need a mitre-box, and to cut mitres well enough for a picture frame you need a *metal* mitre-box. The one we use is the Marples mitre-box shown in **Fig. 6**. This one cuts both 45° and 90° angles and takes mouldings up to 5 cm wide. (There is another Marples model which only cuts 45° angles.) In the bed of the box are two screw holes for fixing it to a work bench. If you don't have a work bench, no matter; screw the box to a length of wood and secure this firmly to a robust table edge with a couple of G-clamps. The picture moulding is laid across the bed of the box and held securely at the cutting angle (either 45° or 90°) by a screw clamp. Two pairs of metal uprights ensure that the tenon-saw blade is kept absolutely upright whilst cutting.

You can buy different sorts of wooden mitre-box but unless you are a budding genius with a tenon-saw you won't cut a really true, upright 45° angle in any of them. The saving in cost isn't worth the anguish caused by a frame that just won't fit together properly.

At the other end of the market, costing hundreds of pounds and hence simply of academic interest, is the cutting equipment used by professional picture framers. This machine, called a Morso cutter, is a foot-operated guillotine with its own measuring device, which shears through the moulding cutting a pair of mitres in one operation.

Tenon-saw For the metal mitre-box described above choose a tenon-saw with a 12-in long blade and 15 teeth/in (Fig. 6). The better quality the saw the better the job it does, so select one by a well-established maker. When you get the saw home, clean the blade with white spirit to remove any protective grease, otherwise it may not slide easily between the uprights on the mitre-box. The blade of the saw is inserted between the uprights from the front, not from the top. Never force the saw when you are cutting, just work it backwards and forwards with an even, easy motion. If the saw does become difficult to use it could be a little blunt, in which case take it to your nearest tool or DIY shop and get it sharpened. You can buy saw sharpeners, but with 15 teeth/in, sharpening is a bit tricky. Always keep a sliver of wood in the cutting groove on the bed of the mitre-box to protect the teeth of the saw, and never ever attempt to cut through a nail in a moulding with a tenon-saw – use a hacksaw instead.

G-clamps (Fig. 4)　As mentioned above a few of these can be useful for holding glued sections together or securing the mitre-box to a work surface.

Vice　The sort of vice shown in **Fig. 7** is fine for holding moulding whilst you join the corners. This is a woodworking vice with two pieces of wood screwed to the jaws to prevent them marking the moulding.

Drill　You require a drill to make pilot holes for the pins that hold the corners of the frame together. A good hand drill **(Fig. 8)** is perfectly adequate, plus some drill bits. The most useful size bits will be 1/32 and 1/16 in.

Hammer　Get yourself a tack hammer **(Fig. 9)**. This is a lightweight hammer and a comfortable weight to wield when pinning corners.

Glue and pins　For glueing corners prior to pinning we recommend Evo-stik Woodworking Adhesive. The most useful sizes of pin are 25, 38 and 44 mm (1, $1\frac{1}{2}$ and $1\frac{3}{4}$ in) panel pins for medium-weight and heavier mouldings, and 25, 19 and 13 mm (1, $\frac{3}{4}$ and $\frac{1}{2}$ in) moulding or veneer pins for lightweight framing. Use a *nail set* or simply a blunt nail to recess the heads of the pins when the frame is complete.

Plastic wood　Use this to fill the holes left after recessing the pin heads. It comes in small tubes, in natural or walnut colour, and can be sanded. The natural colour will take a stain.

Sundries　At some stage you may need *glass paper*, and the extra-fine version, *flour paper*. *Wood stains*, *paints* and *polishes* are covered in Chapter 6.

The method of joining a frame that we describe in Chapter 2 is the traditional one. It is well tried and efficient, not at all difficult to master and requires only the tools mentioned above. However you can buy metal *corner clamps* **(Fig. 10)**.

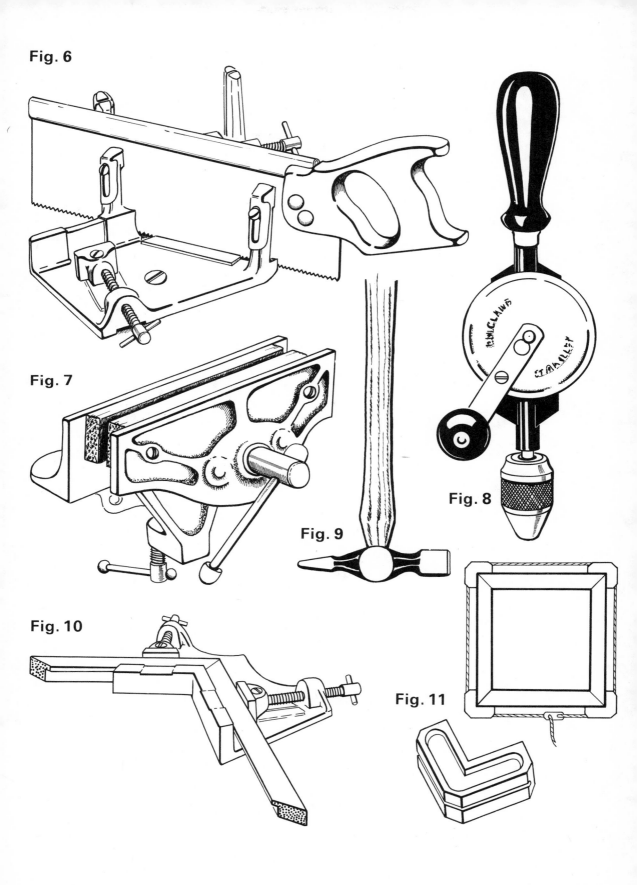

Fig. 6

Fig. 7

Fig. 8

Fig. 9

Fig. 10

Fig. 11

These enable you to force the mitres tightly together after glueing, and you can pin whilst the clamps are still in position. The mitre-box shown on page **15** doubles as a corner clamp, and you can also buy a clamp that looks similar but doesn't have the pillars (Fig. 10). There are other sorts of screw-up clamp too. Another type of corner clamp (very basic) consists of four plastic corners and a cord **(Fig. 11)**. The idea is that you lay the frame on a flat surface, glue the mitres, place the plastic corners in position, then draw the mitres snugly together by tightening the cord around the corners. Later, when the mitres are set, they can be pinned. Both these sorts of clamps work perfectly well, and the metal, screw-type ones can be especially helpful if you're dealing with heavy, unwieldy frames. But on the whole the skill of the professional is well worth acquiring – it is much less fuss, quicker and altogether a more satisfying way of putting smaller frames together.

Mounts

A mount is the cardboard surround given to most watercolours, prints and etchings etc. to both enhance and protect them. The salient feature of mount board is that it is white all the way through so that the bevelled edges of a mount window look clean and uniform. Other types of board often have a middle grey layer which makes an unsightly edge.

Most art shops and many picture framers sell mount board and keep a swatch of samples that you can peruse. It is generally sold in two sizes, Imperial – 81 × 56 cm (32 × 22 in) and Double Imperial – 112 × 81 cm (44 × 32 in).

Coloured mount board usually consists of a white board faced on one side with a paper. Some of the nicest are Canson boards which are faced with papers of the same name. In fact if you can't track down the particular colour board you want, it's a simple business to face your own. You need a sheet of white mount board, the paper that takes your fancy and a can of spray-on gum (Spray Mount) available at most art shops. Follow the instructions for use given on the canister.

If you face your own boards your choice of paper is

fabulous. In plain white there are various watercolour and etching papers, some of them really thick and well textured. For a beautiful range of subtle colours you can't beat Canson paper. It differs in weight and texture – the paper called Mi-teinte is the thickest and most heavily textured, whilst Ingres paper is thinner and smoother with a characteristic line mark in it. Tumbra paper, the Swedish version of Ingres paper, has a distinctive grey fleck in it which is very pleasing. Specialist paper stockists, like the one listed at the end of the book, are a treasure trove of exotic papers, amongst them some exquisite hand-made Japanese papers. At the cheaper end of the scale you can buy gold and silver paper and sugar paper. Sugar paper is extremely cheap but fades very quickly.

If you have a subject of great rarity or value to frame or simply something that you treasure personally and wish to preserve for all time, then ordinary mount board won't do. It tends to absorb acid present in the air and eventually discolours any subject in contact with it. So, for pictures you cherish, use acid-free mount board, also called 'museum' or 'conservation' board.

This board is made from acid-free rag or neutralized wood pulp. One of the main suppliers of acid-free board and paper is given at the end of the book, but try your local art shop or picture framer. If they don't stock it they may be able to order it for you. The largest size board available is about 81 × 115 cm (32 × 45 in), but it does come in several smaller sheets and on the whole works out about twice the cost of ordinary mount board. More information about acid-free board appears on page **49**.

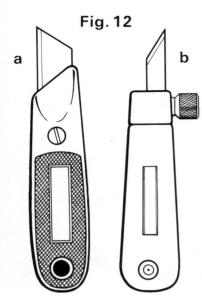

Fig. 12

a

b

Tools for cutting and making mounts

The weapon you use for cutting the bevelled window in the mount is largely a matter of personal preference. You can use an ordinary *Stanley knife* equipped with a No. 5 blade **(Fig. 12a)**, or use a No. 3 blade held in a pad saw handle **(Fig. 12b)**. We find either of these comfortable and efficient to use providing the blades are new and razor sharp. Buy plenty of blades and discard them the moment cutting becomes anything less than easy.

There are special mount cutters on the market, but the

Fig. 13

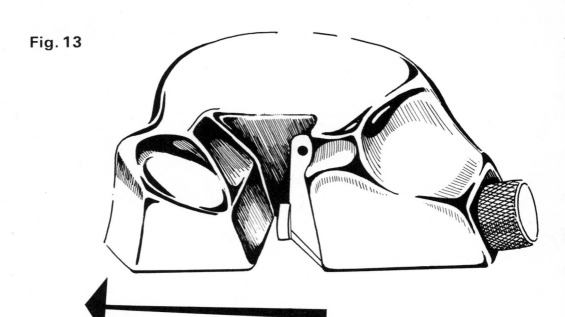

only one within the scope of the amateur's pocket is the sort shown in **Fig. 13**. This is the Dexter *mount cutter*. Exacto make a similar one which is a bit cheaper. In these cutters special replaceable blades (which incidentally are quite expensive) are held securely at an angle and can be set to different depths depending on the thickness of mount board you are cutting. Art shops should stock one of these two cutters.

With both Stanley knife and mount cutter you need a straight edge against which to cut. Now, whether you simply buy a steel ruler or whether you invest in a proper *steel straightedge* depends on the method you use to cut your mounts, how much money you've got to spend and how long-term your picture-framing interest is likely to be. (See page **26** for cutting mounts.) A steel straightedge is thicker and heavier than the ordinary steel ruler and so affords a better and safer edge against which to cut. You can also use it with a glass-cutter. A *set square* is indispensable for marking absolutely square mounts and mount windows. Straight-edges and set squares should be available from most good art shops.

For hinging mounts together you require some *sticky tape*. This can be Sellotape, masking tape or gum strip. For acid-free board make sure you use gum strip, i.e. the type you lick.

Lines around mount windows can easily be drawn with a fountain pen and coloured ink, but if you want to produce lines of different widths you need a *ruling pen* **(Fig. 14a)**. These are quite cheap and well worth having. Some of the thicker inks, like white, black and gold flow easily through a ruling pen but tend to gum up a fountain pen. A ruling pen can also be cleaned quickly, so changing colour is no problem. Watercolour paints diluted with distilled water can be used in a ruling pen too.

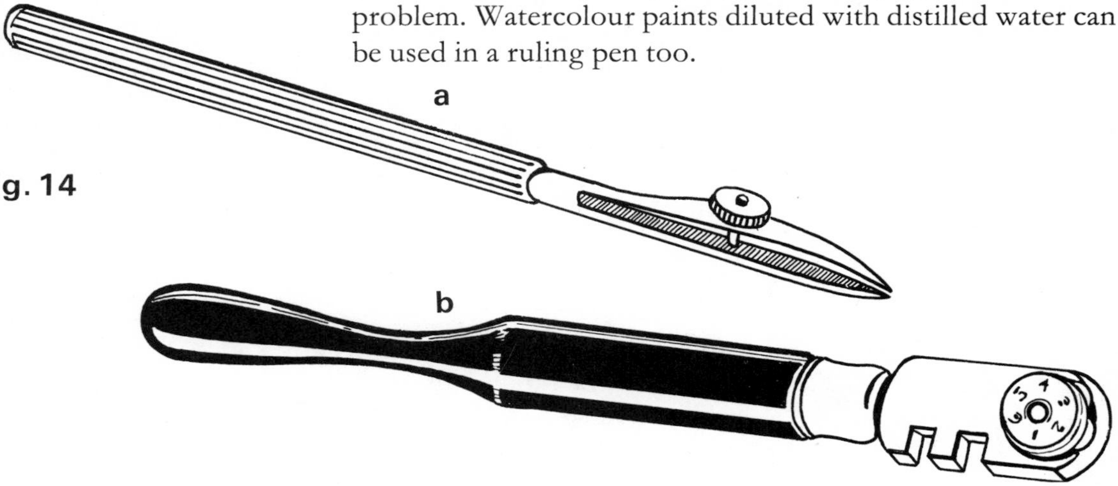

a

Fig. 14

b

Glass

Glass is necessary for a great many frames, so sooner or later you'll probably want to cut your own if it's only a case of cutting down old glass to fit new frames. But have a care and treat glass with respect. Cutting smallish pieces yourself is fine; cutting sizeable pieces is best left to the expert, that is your local glass merchant.

Standard picture glass is 2 mm thick. All glass merchants stock it and sell it by the square foot. If you want glass cut for you, either take the frame along and let the glazier measure it up, or give him the rebate measurements minus a little to make sure the glass will fit.

Most glass merchants also keep non-reflecting glass. This has a sort of textured surface which very effectively checks reflection but at the same time reduces clarity slightly and in our opinion fails to impart to a picture the same 'quality' that ordinary picture glass gives it.

For cutting glass you need two things, a *glass-cutter* with which to score the glass and a *straightedge* against which to run the cutter. The type of cutter in **Fig. 14b** has replaceable steel wheels and is more than adequate. Most glaziers use a diamond-tipped cutter which will outlast any other sort but which is much more expensive. Have some *white spirit* handy in which to dip the cutter. (See page **41** for hints on cutting glass.) If you want to remove the razor-sharp edges of a piece of glass, rub them down with *wet emery cloth*.

As a straight edge you need something rather thicker than the average ruler. A paper-hanger's yard or a carpenter's rule is fine, or of course a steel straightedge. An ordinary ruler resting on a strip of cardboard will do as well. But for large jobs, and especially if you reckon on cutting a lot of glass, a *wooden T-square* is a good investment.

Back boards

Most glazed frames require a firm back. The best material to use is hardboard. Standard thickness hardboard (about 3 mm) is available from most DIY shops and timber yards. Unfortunately rebates on picture mouldings are often quite shallow and by the time glass and mounts are in place, won't accommodate the full thickness of the hardboard back. Ways of coping with this problem are suggested on page **42**. Actually there is a very thin hardboard made (about 2 mm thick) but very few people seem to stock it. You may be able to find some through your local picture framer.

For the sort of glass and clip frame described on page **83** you may prefer to use an extra-thick back board. The high-density hardboard called Masonite is ideal for this and can be bought from most DIY shops and timber yards, as can plywood and chipboard.

Materials for assembling

Back boards are best pinned into the frame with 13 mm ($\frac{1}{2}$ in) *veneer pins* (see Fig. **22** page **42**). Where the back board lies flush with the back of the frame it can be secured with *turnclips* **(Fig. 15a)**. To seal the back of the frame and prevent dust filtering in you also require some *brown gum strip*. Apart from this, all you need are some fixings and wire for hanging the picture.

The most common fixings are *D-rings* **(Fig. 15b)**. If the frame is reasonably wide and stout these can be screwed into the back of the frame. If the frame is narrow they can be riveted to the back board instead. Ask for either screws or rivets when you buy the D-rings. *Screw eyes* or screw rings **(Fig. 15c)** are an alternative to D-rings. They can be bought in various sizes and the smallest of them will screw into the narrowest of frames. To hang the pictures use the special *picture wire* or *cord* available from most art shops, picture framers and DIY shops. Brass picture wire comes in two thicknesses and the heavier gauge should support the weightiest of pictures. If you want a picture secured absolutely flush with the wall use *mirror plates* **(Fig. 15d)**. These can be riveted to a back board or frame back, and screwed to the wall.

Clip and glass frames (see also page **83**) require a number of '*spring clips*' **(Fig. 15e)**. These come in two sizes and the one you need depends on how thick your final assembly of glass, mount and back board is. If you are careful you can put the clips in position and just tap the lugs into the back board with a hammer. A safer method is to make a small hole in the back board to take the lug on each clip, then slide the slips over the edge of the assembly and push the lugs firmly into the holes. If you favour a really thick back board you can use *mirror corners* to hold everything together. These are secured by screwing them into the back board **(Fig. 15f)**. For very large subjects where the weight of glass is pretty substantial, chrome-headed *mirror bolts* **(Fig. 15g)** may be the safest option. In this case get your glazier to drill the holes for the

Fig. 15

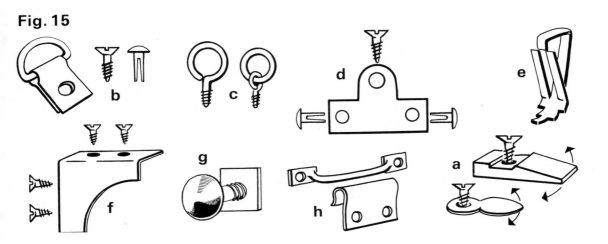

bolts in the corners of the glass. The corresponding holes in mount and back board you can make yourself.

Any strut-back frame, that is the sort that sits on shelves and mantelpieces, requires a fixing for the strut. This can be an ordinary small *cabinet hinge* plus a ribbon tie (see Fig. 10 page **89**), or the *clip-on fixing* shown in **Fig. 15h**. Both should be attached to a hardboard back board and strut with rivets.

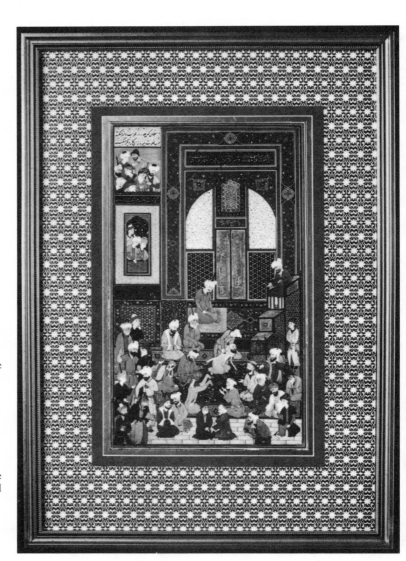

'Scandal in a Mosque', reproduction of a Persian miniature by Shaykh Zadeh, 25 × 15 cm. Patterned mounts can be dangerous, but where the subject is highly intricate and invites close scrutiny a decorative border becomes part of that intricacy. In this case the patterned mount implies a whole world of intrigue contemporary with the events depicted by Zadeh. A plain mount would have disembodied them, placed them in a vacuum. Note however the importance of the visual break between the picture and the mount. This was achieved by backing the picture with dark blue paper before tipping it on to the patterned mount.

CHAPTER 2

Making a straightforward glazed frame with a mount

In this chapter we discuss the making of the traditional type of glazed frame, with a mount, from start to finish. This is the sort of frame commonly used for watercolours, prints, drawings, engravings, photographs . . . anything which needs protection and subtle flattery. As will be seen from photograph A on page **34** and B, C and D on page **35**, there may be several acceptable treatments for a given subject. In this case the subject is a watercolour on cartridge paper, fairly vivid as watercolours go, with plenty of free space around the quietly lurking trout.

Every painting has its special atmosphere. If you are sensitive to it you are likely to create a frame which 'works', a setting which gently enhances it. Every genre – watercolours, drawings, oil paintings, posters – has intrinsic qualities which make certain treatments more apt than others, and these are discussed under the relevant headings in Chapters 3 to 6.

Traditionally watercolours are framed in a mount under glass (Fig. 1a on page **9**). A mount is not simply a convenient way of creating space between the edge of the painting and the frame. It has a practical purpose too, to prevent the glass touching the paint surface, and it is made before the frame. The sequence of operations necessary to frame our trout, as displayed opposite, was:

1 Decide on the colour, window size and approximate area of the mount
2 Cut the mount front and mount back to approximate size
3 Cut the window in the mount front and decorate it with ink and wash lines

4　Hinge the mount front to the mount back and attach the painting to the mount back

5　Decide on a suitable frame and the length of moulding required

6　Sand and stain the moulding (only necessary on raw wood or DIY mouldings)

7　Cut the mount to the exact rebate size

8　Cut the frame to rebate size and join it; wax or French polish the finished frame (not necessary with ready-finished mouldings)

9　Cut the glass to rebate size and clean it thoroughly

10　Cut a hardboard back to the rebate size and put the glass, mount and back into the rebate

11　Pin the picture back in place and dust seal it with gum strip

12　Attach picture hooks and wire

Stages 1 to 4 can be omitted of course if the visual advantages of a mount are not required. But in order to separate the painting from the glass, narrow strips of mount board, hidden by the rebate, should be placed between the glass and the painting.

Making the mount

It being an aesthetically safer proposition to work from the painting outwards to the frame rather than from the frame inwards to the painting, the mount rather than the frame is one's first concern.

Colour considerations come first, not only because the colour you choose for the mount front should echo some facet of the painting's personality but because it influences the proportions of the mount. Over and above the emotional overtones of various colours, pale mounts make a gentle, airy transition between painting and frame, and dark mounts have a strongly confining effect. An unadorned cream mount for our lurking trout would have been acceptable, but rather uninteresting; the ink and wash lines, which make it into what is called a 'French' mount, gently direct the eye into the painting without disrupting the spacious feeling of the whole.

How much of the painting should show through the

mount window? This area is called the 'sight area' and the proportions of the whole frame ultimately depend on it. Our trout looked best in an almost square window which left a little space between the green weeds and the edges of the window. Two L-shaped pieces of paper are a great help in deciding on the exact sight area **(Fig. 1)**, but allow an extra 3 mm on both dimensions because the bevelled edge of the window takes up roughly that width.

Next, how much space should there be between the edge of the window and the frame? Quite a lot for small paintings and less for larger ones is a good rule of thumb. A medium-sized painting like our trout (30×31 cm) would have looked rather cramped in a border of anything less than about 10 cm. Convention, based on the fact that the eye perceives bottom borders as narrower than they really are, dictates that the bottom border should be a little wider, by 20% say, than the top border. If the side borders are the same width as the top border the overall proportions, in the opinion of those who believe they have an 'eye' and those who freely confess they haven't, are perceived as pleasing and satisfying **(Fig. 2)**. Again use two L-shaped pieces of paper to help you decide how wide the mount borders should be.

Fig. 1

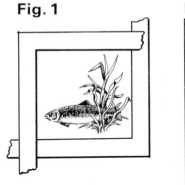

Fig. 2

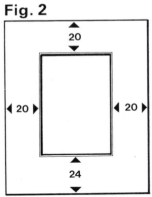

Fig. 3

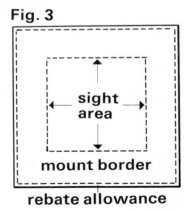

The rebate of the frame will hide the edges of the mount by 5 to 10 mm. This is why, at this stage, before you have chosen an appropriate moulding for the frame, you should over-allow on the area of the mount **(Fig. 3)**.

The next operation is to cut a piece of mount board to the approximate area decided on, using a set square, a good straightedge and a sharp craft knife. Cut a mount back, out of cheaper or thinner card if you like, exactly the same size.

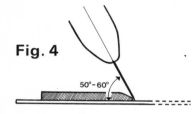

Fig. 4

50°–60°

Pencil in the outline of the window on the front of the mount front ready for cutting.

We find that the easiest method of cutting bevelled mount windows is the one which requires the least equipment: a steel rule or straightedge and a Stanley knife. Using the rule to guide your knife, score lightly but firmly along your pencilled lines, holding the knife at an angle between 50° and 60° **(Fig. 4)** and pulling it towards you. End each score exactly in the window corners. With or without the rule, whichever feels more comfortable, score lightly along each line again, still holding the knife at the same angle. Repeat, each time scoring deeper and at the same angle, until you have cut right through. If you have not cut right into the corners you may need to slip the blade, at the correct angle, into them so that the middle lifts out cleanly. A gentle rub with a piece of flour paper will smooth away any unevenness or fuzziness.

Problems can be avoided by having a really sharp blade in your knife, and a clean, flat work surface (such as a spare piece of thick card). If your blade is blunt the cut will feel bumpy. Mount cutting by this method is a skill well worth acquiring. Practise cutting bigger and bigger windows in a spare piece of mount board and see how fast you improve.

In our experience cutting satisfactory mounts with the sort of mount cutter illustrated on page **18** takes just as much practice as using a knife and straightedge, and there are several drawbacks despite the advantages of having the blade firmly held at a constant angle and depth. First, the straight-edge or rule used to guide the cutter must be securely fixed at one end to prevent it slipping sideways as one pushes the cutter along it; this can be done by hammering a peg or nail through the hole in the end of the rule and into the work surface **(Fig. 5)**. Second, the straightedge must be fairly thick or the edge of the cutter is liable to slip over it, causing the blade to wander off the cutting line. Lastly, it is quite difficult to cut through acid-free board, of a more solid consistency than ordinary mount board, in one go, and the whole point of using a mount cutter is to cut right through board in one go. Mount cutters come with full instructions on how to use them of course. However, we strongly recommend that you try the knife and straightedge method first.

Fig. 5

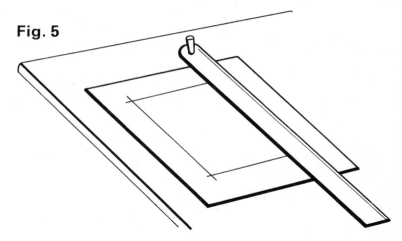

Hints on decorating mounts with ink and wash lines are given on page 52.

To complete the mount, hinge the mount front and back together with gum strip, Sellotape or masking tape. Having positioned the painting on the mount back so that the desired area shows through the window, use two stamp hinges or two small pieces of double-sided Sellotape to attach it to the mount back **(Fig. 6)**. These should be as close as possible to the top edge of the painting.

Fig. 6

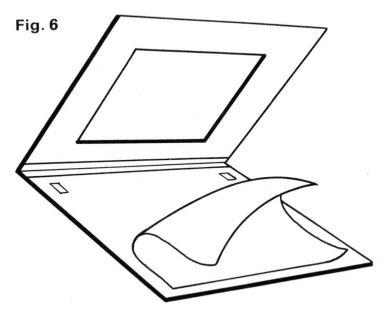

Making the frame

It is all too easy to overpower and destroy the subtlety of a watercolour with too hefty or too dark a frame. That said, a wide frame is quite acceptable if it is in a pale-coloured wood. Conversely a dark frame can look very dignified provided it is fairly narrow. Choosing frames for watercolours is gone into in more detail in Chapter 3. The moulding we chose for the 'Trout' on page **34** is one available in many DIY shops. Before it was mitred it was sanded smooth and stained, using spirit-based wood stain diluted with white spirit. Stains and finishes for unfinished and made-up mouldings are discussed in Chapter 8.

First of all, what length of moulding do you need? With expensive mouldings, sold by the foot, it pays to work this out fairly accurately. The formula for doing so is:

Perimeter of mount	+	**Eight times the width of the moulding**	+	**Small cutting allowance**

For the 'Trout', as framed on page **34,** this worked out as follows:

$$(50 + 50 + 54 + 54) + (8 \times 4) + 20\,cm = 260\,cm$$

If for any reason, such as fitting it into your car or getting on a bus with it, it is impractical to buy the whole length you require in one piece, ask the supplier to cut it exactly in half. This is the safest option because it allows you to get one long and one short side out of each half.

We have already said that metal mitre-boxes cut better mitres than the wooden sort. But it is important that the box should be firmly screwed or clamped to the edge of the work surface, which should stand firm and not wobble. A really sharp tenon-saw is also essential. Putting a slip of wood in the saw groove in the bed of the box will prevent the teeth grating against the metal. All makes of metal mitre-box give cutting instructions and recommend a suitable length of saw and number of teeth per inch.

There are three musts for positioning the moulding in the box ready for cutting:

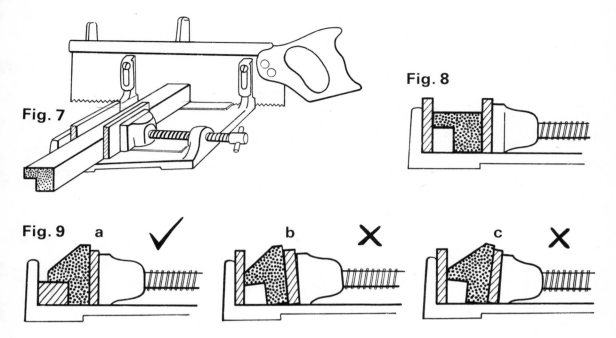

Fig. 7

Fig. 8

Fig. 9   a ✓   b ✗   c ✗

1   Always clamp the moulding with the rebate side away from you **(Fig. 7)**

2   Always insert a piece of thin wooden batten between the box and the sides of the moulding **(Fig. 8)** so that the metal of the box does not mark the moulding

3   Always make sure the bottom of the moulding is resting completely flat on the bed of the box when the clamp is fully screwed up. To achieve verticality it may be necessary to support the rebate side of the moulding on a small piece of wood which you know to be perfectly square **(Fig. 9a)**. This counteracts the tendency of the clamp to push the moulding out of the vertical as you screw it tight **(Fig. 9b, c)**. Look along the side of the moulding to check for verticality – the human eye is capable of detecting even the tiniest deviation. If the moulding isn't vertical in relation to the bed of the box when you make a 45° cut, the cut will be distorted so that either top or bottom of the joined corner will gape. Very nasty . . .

Practise cutting mitres on spare pieces of moulding before you attempt the operation for real.

The first four cuts you make in a length of moulding require next to no measuring. Make two mitre cuts exactly in

Fig. 10

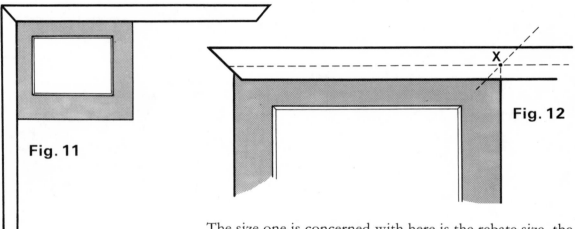

the middle of the length, and then mitre the other end of each half **(Fig. 10)**. You now have two pieces of moulding the same length with useable mitres at both ends. Out of each half you then proceed to cut one long side and one short side.

Now is the time to check whether your rebate allowance on the mount is correct. Butt the cut halves of the moulding together to make an L and slip the mount under the rebate **(Fig. 11)**. Could the space between the sight edge of the frame and the edge of the mount window be narrower, or is it just right? Having trimmed the mount to the exact rebate size required, you are ready to cut the four sides of the frame.

Fig. 11

Fig. 12

The size one is concerned with here is the rebate size, the size that will exactly fit the trimmed mount. This is best determined practically rather than by calculation. Butt one of the moulding lengths against one of the long sides of the mount so that the corner of the mount is a millimetre or so inside the vertical edge of the rebate. The mitre cut which makes the other end of this long side must intersect a point, point **X** in **Fig. 12**, directly in line with the edge of the mount and exactly the rebate width away from the sight edge. Mark point **X** with a pencil. When you have made your cut it should just be visible on the cut portion of the moulding. This applies to all such pencil guide marks. Place the long side you have just cut back-to-back with the other uncut half of the moulding and mark a point **P** on it. If your moulding

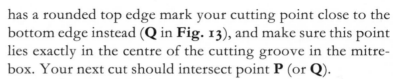

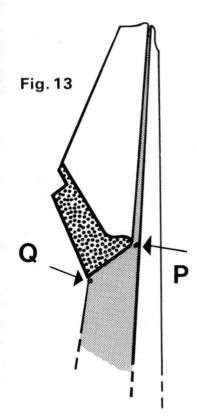

Fig. 13

Q

P

has a rounded top edge mark your cutting point close to the bottom edge instead (**Q** in **Fig. 13**), and make sure this point lies exactly in the centre of the cutting groove in the mitre-box. Your next cut should intersect point **P** (or **Q**).

You should now have an identical pair of long sides and can proceed to cut the two short sides by the same method. Naturally it is most important that pairs of sides should be of identical length. Even a small discrepancy will show up in a small frame when it comes to joining. Discrepancies of less than about 3 mm are difficult to correct, because 3 mm is about the thinnest sliver that can be sawn off in the mitre-box. It might be better to trim, say, 5 mm off the width or length of the mount and recut the offending pair of sides.

A note of encouragement here. Most picture framers make up frames to fit existing pictures – this is why we have described how to make a frame to fit a mount. However, you may find it easier to make your frame first, more or less to the desired size, and then cut your mount to fit.

Joining a frame is a very quick and satisfying operation, but do practise first with the trial mitre pieces cut earlier. We favour glueing and pinning simultaneously, making two L's first, then joining the L's together to make the rectangle **(Fig. 14)**. Glue on its own does not really make a strong or durable enough join. Nor do we find it necessary, with the simultaneous glueing and pinning method, to use corner clamps (described on page **16**), though such aids are indispensable if one is of the 'glue first, pin later' school or if you have a large or weighty frame to deal with.

The tools and materials needed for joining are a vice, firmly clamped to the table edge; a hand drill with a bit slightly smaller in diameter than the pins being used; a tack hammer; a nailset or a blunted nail for sinking the heads of the pins below the surface of the moulding; plus of course Evo-stik adhesive, pins of a reasonable length (15-mm veneer pins for thin mouldings, 25-mm panel or moulding pins for thicker mouldings) and plastic wood of the appropriate colour for filling the holes made by recessing the pin heads.

It is perfectly possible, accidentally, to join both long sides or both short sides together! To prevent such mishaps place the frame pieces on the work table as they will appear when the frame is joined. Please note that the following instruc-

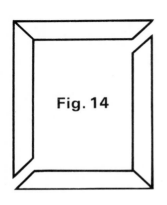

Fig. 14

tions are for right-handers; just reverse everything if you are left-handed.

Start by drilling two holes in one end of each piece of moulding, working methodically round the frame (see arrows in **Fig. 15**). Put each piece in the vice the same way round and drill your pairs of holes nearer to the bottom edge of the moulding than the front **(Fig. 16)**. Optimum hole

Fig. 15

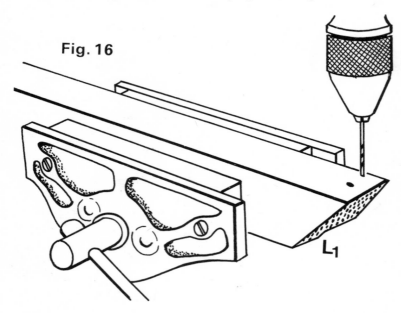

Fig. 16

Photographed opposite are just a few of the literally hundreds of mouldings it is possible to track down or make yourself. Nos.1 to 25 are proper rebated picture mouldings and nos. 26 to 32 are mouldings made up from DIY timber mouldings. Nos. 33 and 34 are two of the most commonly available ready-made slips. Plain wood mouldings can of course be stained or painted any colour you like.

1 Shallow, stepped profile moulding with plain gilt beading and cream sight edge
2 Moulding with centre band of gilt and grey (colour picture **C**)
3 Flat profile moulding with four rows of plain beading, ramin stained and French polished (colour picture **G**)
4 Shallow scoop with plain beading, ramin stained and waxed

5 White and buff finished deep scoop with linen band and gilt sight edge
6 Half round with stepped sight edge, pine waxed (photograph page **46**)
7 Same as 4 but not so wide (colour picture **A**)
8 Reverse shape, maple veneer on pine (colour picture **N**)
9 Reverse ogee shape, oak stained and waxed (colour picture **M**)
10 Planewood moulding with grey shading and gold sight edge
11 Narrow plain beaded moulding, oak stained and waxed
12 Flat profile with black lacquer finish and fluted gilt sight edge
13 Hogarth moulding
14 Narrow black cushion (photograph page **47**)
15 Wide gilt spoon-type moulding with close ribbing
16 A canvas moulding, gilt and plaster 'bamboo' with black detail

17 Plain flat canvas moulding with gilt finish
18 Narrow plain beaded moulding with gilt and 'bole' finish
19 Narrow gold finish moulding with plain and fancy beading (photograph page **22**)
20 Flat canvas moulding with aluminium finish (colour picture **E**)
21 Narrow flat, silver gilt (colour picture **Q**)
22 Plain box moulding, ramin waxed
23 Narrow box moulding, ramin waxed
24 Narrow cushion moulding, oak stained and waxed (colour picture **M**)
25 Narrow flat moulding, oak stained and waxed
Nos. 26 to 32 are mouldings made up from DIY timber sections:
26 Moulding for a floating frame made from two rectangular sections of ramin, one stained, one painted
27 Wide pine architrave moulding with a pine rebate section, stained black (colour picture **L**)
28 Same as 27, lightly stained and waxed (colour picture **D**)
29 A canvas moulding made from pine panel moulding and pine rebate section, stained and waxed (colour picture **H**)
30 Flat moulding made from two rectangular sections of mahogany, stained and varnished (colour picture **F**)
31 Simple spoon shape using scotia moulding for the front and glass beading for the rebate, stained and waxed (colour picture **B**)
32 Same as 31, painted red (colour picture **O**)
33 Flat gilt slip with fluted edge (colour pictures **H**, **G** and **L**)
34 Linen-covered slip, sloping profile

A 'Trout' by Martin Knowlden, watercolour, 32 × 30 cm. The frame used here was made from a shallow 'scoop' type ramin moulding, lightly stained and waxed. The wash line on the mount creates an unobtrusive frame-within-a-frame effect and echoes the greens and browns of the subject. Three alternative treatments of the same subject appear opposite.

B

C

D

B A double mount, with pale green predominating. Had the brown been predominant the effect would have been much murkier. The window in the green mount is approx. 1.5 cm wider all round than the window in the brown one. The frame was made from two sections of DIY pine moulding stained mid-brown and waxed.

C A more formal environment achieved with a dark green mount (dark colours are always more enclosing in their effect). The glint of gold in the frame and the simple white wash line on the mount avoid stuffiness though.

D The 'Trout' is displayed here in a very wide frame made from two sections of DIY pine moulding, lightly stained and waxed. Narrow strips of mount board, hidden by the rebate, keep the paint surface away from the glass.

E An example of a multi-windowed mount. Usually one avoids making bold distracting statements with mounts, but here the subject, several sets of stamps, has insufficient impact to create a picture on its own. The frame is a flat aluminium-finish moulding, chosen because of its neutrality, the mount and stamps looking 'busy' enough without further embellishment.

E

F 'Celestial Planisphere of the Northern and Southern Hemisphere', c. 1700, by Carel Allard (Amsterdam), reproduction, 30 × 71 cm. Note how the pale green mount picks up the greens in the subject (a pale blue mount would have looked slightly chilly) and how the sight area includes a narrow band of white all round the map. This strip of white gives a breathing space between the map and the mount and also makes the colours of the map appear brighter. For the frame we used two sections of mahogany stained a rich red-brown and sealed with French polish. The brass 'military chest' corners are not necessary structurally but they bring out the scientific flavour of the subject. Fine brass instruments were associated with most cartographic endeavours up until the nineteenth century.

F

G

G A small sepia photo portrait (15 × 12 cm) of an Edwardian 'belle', set off by a wide mid-brown frame (a ramin moulding stained and French polished). The oval mount is a double one, using thin gold card for the smaller window and fabric-covered mount board for the larger. The gold slip, the moiré silk and the very ovalness of the mount conjure up an era more gracious than our own. Having considerable sentimental value the picture stands on a desk top, supported by a strut back.

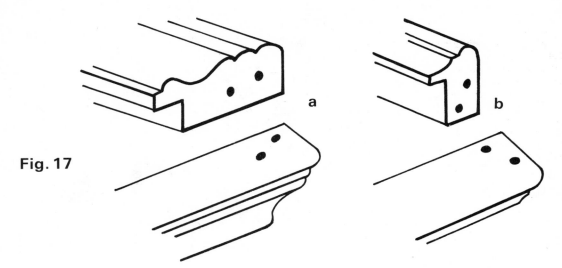

Fig. 17

positions depend on the shape of the moulding, of course **(Fig. 17a, b)**; but try to ensure that the holes emerge more or less in the middle of the mitred surface, not too near the front of the moulding or too near the rebate edge. Having drilled all your holes, use a razor-sharp knife to carefully trim off the whiskers on all but the face edge of the moulding.

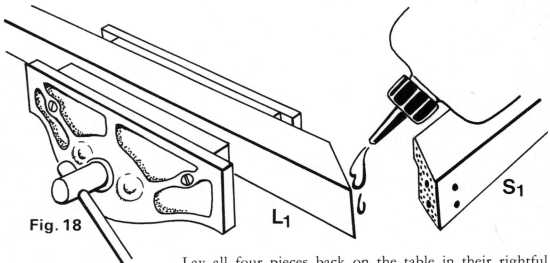

Fig. 18 L_1 S_1

Lay all four pieces back on the table in their rightful positions. Now take one long side, L_1 in **Fig. 18**, and clamp it tightly in the vice face up with the rebate side away from you and the undrilled end poking out on the right. Smear this end with Evo-stik. Don't be too liberal or the glue will only squeeze out of the join and have to be wiped off with a damp cloth. Butt the end of the corresponding short side, S_1, against the glued end of L_1 so that it sticks out slightly as in

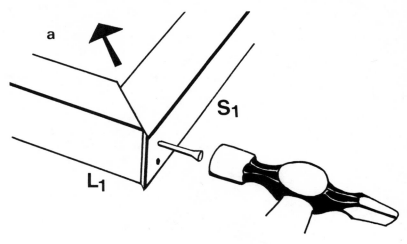

Fig. 19

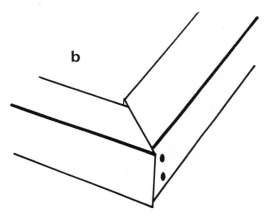

Fig. 19a. As you hammer in the first pin, S_1 will move in the direction of the arrow. If it doesn't stick out to start with you'll end up with a join looking like **Fig. 19b**. Make sure that the face edges of the mitres are exactly level and well pressed together before you drive in the first pin. Now hammer home the second pin. If you are a right-hander you wield the hammer in your right hand and hold the corners together with your left (**Fig. 20** shows the correct holding position).

Repeat the operation with L_2 and S_2 so that you have two L pieces. It is as well to let the glue set (about 15 minutes) before you join the two Ls together. This you do in just the same way as before, except that this time the short sides will be gripped in the vice. Use books or small pieces of wood to support the rest of the frame at the required height.

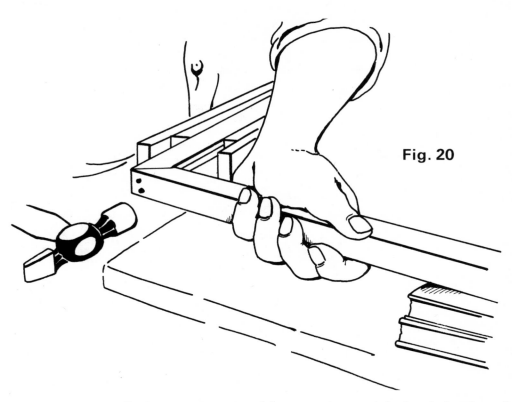

Fig. 20

It always seems more labour-saving to sink the pin heads and fill the holes with plastic wood as one goes along rather than making a separate operation of it. Once the plastic wood has hardened, carefully sand it flush with the surface of the moulding and sand off any fuzziness at the corners or backs of the joins. Use very fine glass paper so as not to damage the surface of the moulding. Traces of sanding, and the colour of natural plastic wood, can of course be disguised by rubbing them with a little wood stain, well worked into a soft cloth.

If you need to, wax or French polish the frame. Both of these finishing methods are described in Chapter 8.

Glazing

A piece of glass cut to the proper size should not rattle around in the rebate, so although the edge of the glass is hidden by the rebate it should be cut accurately, to a tolerance of, say, 1 mm on both dimensions.

Handling large pieces of glass is most unnerving, in fact disastrous unless you have proper transport and storage, and a huge, flat, padded surface for cutting it on. Two-millimetre picture glass is horribly fragile and nowadays quite expensive. Our advice is that you let the glazier cut the larger pieces (50 × 50 cm and upwards), confining yourself to cutting small pieces or cutting down pieces taken from old frames.

There is nothing more frustrating than finding a piece of glass is a hair's breadth too big for a rebate. Sometimes you can sand the inside of the rebate to make the glass fit, but why cause problems for yourself? Take the finished frame to the glazier – he prefers it this way, having learned, probably after years of experience, to distrust customers' rebate measurements. First, he'll check whether your frame is square. Probably one end will be a millimetre or so longer than the other, almost inevitable with larger frames. He'll then measure one dimension and cut a piece of glass the same width. Then he'll slip the glass into the rebate and cut off the excess at the other end without removing the glass from the frame **(Fig. 21)**. He simply sees where the inside edge of the rebate comes, places his straightedge just inside it and cuts. That's expertise for you. The casual twist of the fingers and thumb of the right hand as he snaps the glass cleanly along the score line is a treat to watch.

This is the best procedure to follow if you are cutting glass yourself. However, to start with it would be wise to make the last cut on the flat, rather than with the glass propped on the edge of the rebate. Use a felt-tip pen to mark both ends of the cut.

Fig. 21

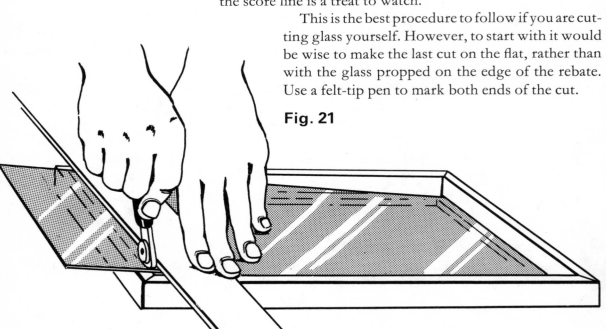

For cutting glass at home you need a completely flat, clean, non-slip work surface, a heavy straightedge (glaziers use a special T-square) and the sort of glass-cutter described on page **19**. Double-sided Sellotape is excellent for preventing both glass and straightedge from slipping while you cut. Dipping the glass-cutter in white spirit before each cut helps the wheel to run freely and also keeps it sharp. A felt-tip pen is ideal for marking guide lines (white spirit will remove felt-tip ink).

Align the straightedge with your felt-tip marks. Rest the cutter against it as close as possible to the far edge of the glass. Now pull the cutter towards you, right to the edge of the glass nearest you, pressing firmly but not attempting to gouge through the glass. The cutter should be held as shown in Fig. 21. Score once, and once only. Overscoring only results in a ragged break or cracks racing in unwanted directions.

To snap the glass along the score line lift it slightly off the table with your left hand (assuming again that you are right-handed), holding the glass just to the left of the score line. With the fingers and thumb of your right hand (thumb on top, index and middle finger underneath), hold the glass just to the right of the score line and give a decisive clockwise twist. The glass should break cleanly along the score line. If the glass doesn't snap off easily, use the glass-cutter to tap underneath the score line at either end. This produces a crack along the score line and should allow the glass to be easily broken along it.

Buy a piece of glass to practise cutting and snapping. When you can snap off 10-cm widths cleanly, try snapping off narrower widths. Small 'thorns' along edges can be bitten off with square-nosed pliers, but if your snapping and cutting is competent this should not be necessary. Edges can be smoothed with wet emery cloth if desired but this is not really necessary where the edges are to be hidden by a rebate.

Assembling

It is most important to clean both sides of the glass thoroughly before slotting it into the rebate. Warm water with a few drops of washing-up liquid in it makes the best cleaning solution. Rub it over the glass with a sponge and then rinse the glass under the tap and dry it with a clean tea towel. In our experience, commercial window-cleaning products, paraffin and methylated spirits, leave a faint film on the glass.

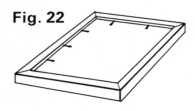

Fig. 22

Remove all specks from the mount face and place it face down on top of the glass. The quicker one marries the mount to the glass the less chance there is of dust and fluff getting trapped between them. The sandwich is completed by a piece of hardboard at the back, cut to the rebate size. The contents of the rebate – glass, mount with the painting inside it, hardboard back – are held in place with veneer pins, two or three per side, driven into the rebate **(Fig. 22)**. This assumes of course that the rebate is deeper than the sandwich. If it isn't the veneer pins must be hammered into the back of the frame, fairly close to the edge of the rebate, and bent over so that their heads touch the hardboard **(Fig. 23a)**. Bend them over with the closed head of a pair of pliers. Don't hammer the heads into the hardboard – ten to one you'll break the glass. Where the hardboard lies flush with the back of the frame there are two solutions; hold it in place with turnclips **(Fig. 23b)** or plane the edges of the hardboard and hammer veneer pins into the rebate as shown in **Fig. 23c**.

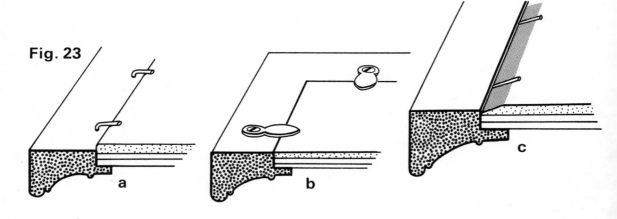

Fig. 23

a   b   c

Last of all, the tiny gap between the frame and the hardboard back is dust sealed **(Fig. 24)** with brown gum strip of a suitable width. This has to be thoroughly wetted or it will not stick, so run a damp sponge over the gummed side, stick it in place and then go over the back with the sponge. Though unconventional, masking tape works just as well.

Hanging

Picture hooks (see page **21**) should be attached to the back of the frame not quite one third of the way down **(Fig. 25)**. Any further down and the top of the picture will hang away from the wall. Make sure the screws or nails you use to attach the hooks are long enough to secure them firmly but not so long that they pierce the front of the moulding.

Fig. 26

Fig. 24

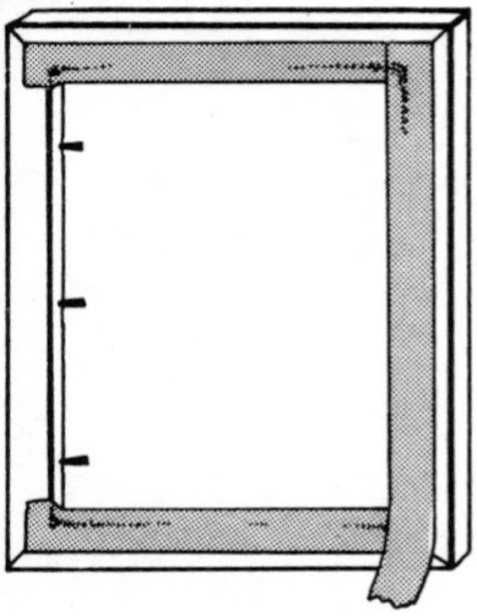

Fig. 25

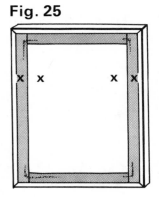

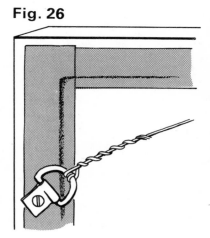

Obviously the wire should not be so slack that the wall hook shows at the top of the picture. When fully stretched it should come within a centimetre or two of the top. Wind the free ends of the wire twice round the D-rings and at least half a dozen times around each end of the wire **(Fig. 26)**. Give the wire a good sustained pull to make sure it will take the strain when you hang the picture up.

Alternative frames for the 'Trout'

Three alternatives for the 'Trout' appear on page **35** and below. In B the picture is given a double mount (described on page **51**) with a plain spoon-type frame made from two pieces of pine stained and waxed. The whole effect is less airy and light-hearted than A on page **34**, better suited to slightly more sombre surroundings. Treatment C is much more formal and severe than A or B, an impression created by the dark tone of the mount, with its classic single white wash line, and the generally dark frame with its gold detail. It has the effect of immobilizing the fish, presenting it more as a trophy than as a living thing. This is the sort of picture that would be more in tune with an entrance hall or study than a quiet living room.

Treatment D on the other hand is cheerfully informal. Small strips of card in the rebate separate the painting from the glass (see Fig. **2** on page **49**) and the frame was made from two pieces of pine moulding, very lightly stained and waxed. It is in this incarnation that our obliging trout now hangs, aptly enough in a friend's kitchen where it provides culinary inspiration.

CHAPTER 3

Watercolours, prints, drawings and engravings

Any picture which has sentimental or monetary value deserves to be framed under glass. Oils, because they are sometimes varnish-sealed, and acrylics, because they are wipeable, stand up better to the grease and grime floating about in our urban air, but a watercolour, drawing, print or engraving can deteriorate very rapidly if exposed to the air. Dust impregnates and darkens the paper. Moisture in the air at best causes wrinkling and at worst encourages the growth of mildew and those little brown spots of mould known in the trade as 'foxing'. Humidity is one of the arch enemies of all works of art. Putting a picture in a frame behind glass only partially prevents its effects. The best preventive is a fairly dry, well ventilated atmosphere. Dust on the other hand can be kept out for many years by sealing the back of the frame. Never hang pictures, especially watercolours or colour prints and reproductions, in positions where they are in strong sunlight; their colours will inevitably fade.

Since by their nature watercolours, prints, engravings and drawings demand slightly different treatment we will be discussing each in turn later in this chapter. But first let's explore the options open to the amateur framer in two areas, mounts and frames.

Mounts

If a lot of space seems to have been devoted to mounts in the previous chapter it is because the immediate juxtaposition of picture and frame is seldom satisfying. Imagine for a moment what the astrological map, F on page 36, or the child's poster painting, J on page 70, would look like without any space between their edges and their frames. Also, compare

Self portrait by Egon Schiele,
reproduction of a drawing,
30 × 23 cm. These two approaches
to the same subject allow different
amounts of 'breathing space' in the
mount. The smaller frame has the
effect of bringing the subject close,
the larger of distancing it. The
frames, the smaller much less
dignified than the larger, add stylistic
weight to this impression.

the 'breathing space' left around the two Egon Schiele self-portraits above.

The conventional relationship of 'sight area' (the area of the picture one wants to be visible) to mount area is explained and illustrated opposite, but one is not obliged to place a subject symmetrically in its mount or even to echo its proportions. The square Nicholson golfer print opposite looks just as good, if not better, in its long frame than its companion in its square frame. The cartoon opposite provided a good excuse for mount 'humour', with the window cut way off-centre.

A mount is a way of creating a comfortable amount of space, space of the right colour and texture, between the picture and the frame. As a rule of thumb the smaller the picture area the bigger the mount can afford to be. For very small subjects a mount several times the dimensions of the sight area may be the most pleasing solution.

Nor does a mount have to be the hinged affair with a bevel-edged window in the front as shown in **Fig. 1a** (page 48). It can be, quite simply, a piece of card larger than the picture with the picture fixed in the middle of it, or 'tipped on' in

The final proportions of a frame do not have to follow those of its subject. These two reproductions of woodcuts by William Nicholson illustrate the point. Both can take the severity of a black frame, having such a lot of solid black in them to start with, and both require a reasonable amount of 'air' around them. Though the boxing print is quite acceptable in its squarish frame, with a mount which obeys the equal-width-top-and-sides-and-a-bit-more-at-the-bottom convention, the golfer print looks more comfortable in its longer frame. This is personal taste perhaps but it may have something to do with the fact that we are all more accustomed to seeing pictures which are oblong rather than square. For both mounts we used the same ivory mount board, very close in colour to the stock on which the subjects are printed.

Cartoon by Hector Breeze, ('Before we converted this place it used to be a tram') 7 × 10 cm. One way of emphasising the quirkiness of the cartoonist's vision—an off-centre mount window. Note that the subject has a double mount, the first of paper, in a fairly light tone, and the second of mount board in a much darker tone. This is a glass/mount/backing sandwich held together with spring clips.

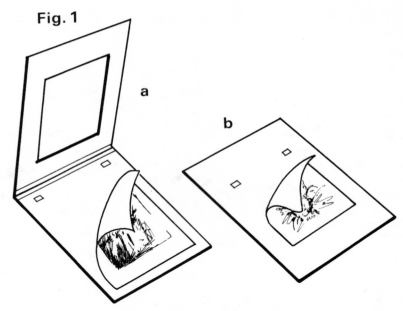

Fig. 1

a

b

framer's jargon **(Fig. 1b)**. Single mounts like this have just the same space-creating effect as the hinged window type. But whatever the type of mount used the picture should be held in place by its top edge only, using two stamp hinges or two small pieces of double-sided Sellotape. One can use paper, provided it is fairly thick, to attach the picture to, but mount board is better.

Mount board

Mount board comes in many colours and in various thicknesses up to about 2.5 mm, but as the thickness increases so does the price. You'll find the widest choice of colours exists in ordinary thickness board, about 1.25 mm. To create a very deep bevelled window of course it would be perfectly feasible to stick two or more pieces of mount board together. Ordinary mount board is white on one side and faced with coloured paper on the other. It should also be white or off-white all the way through, so that it gives a nice white edge when cut.

There are any number of papers (Canson, Arches, cartridge, sugar paper, various types of embossed papers, marbled endpapers, wrapping papers) which can be used to 'face' white mount board to achieve the colour, texture or pattern required. 'Facing' involves spraying the entire surface of the mount board with Spray Mount (a spray-on gum available from most art shops) and firmly smoothing the paper on to it all over. Don't be tempted to use wallpaper paste; the mount board will wrinkle and separate into its constituent layers.

Acid-free mount board, strongly recommended for old or valuable subjects, comes in various thicknesses of cream and white up to about 2.5 mm, and in a limited range of browns, greys, etc. of a standard thickness (around 1.25 mm). It is the same colour on both sides, and white, cream, grey, brown, etc. all the way through.

As its name implies, acid-free board contains no acids which can react with moisture in the air causing stains to appear on parts of the picture resting against it. If you are making a hinged mount of acid-free board, use acid-free for the back as well as the front or the purpose of using acid-free materials is defeated. Use white or brown gum strip (virtually acid-free) to hinge the back and front together. The important thing is that all materials likely to come into contact with the painting should be acid-free. One can face the front of the mount window with paper or fabric which is not acid-free, or make a second, larger, mount window (a double mount, see page **51**) out of ordinary mount board and still observe this stricture. If the picture is to be tipped on to acid-free board, use strips of acid-free board in the rebate to keep the picture away from the glass.

Single mounts

As we have just implied it is bad practice to cram a tipped-on subject directly against the glass. So with single-mounts it is customary to insert strips of mount board between the mount and glass so that they are hidden by the rebate **(Fig. 2)**. The Persian miniature on page **22** has been given single-mount treatment, though in this case the mount board was faced with patterned paper, and the picture backed with dark blue Canson paper before being tipped on.

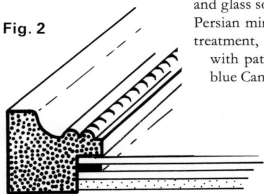

Fig. 2

Hinged mounts

This type of mount offers greater creative latitude than the single type. First of all the front of the mount, the piece with the window in it, does not have to be made of mount board. A thickish paper would be adequate in some cases. Nor does the window have to be rectangular. In the photo portrait on page **36** the mount window is oval and made of thin gold card.

Fig. 3

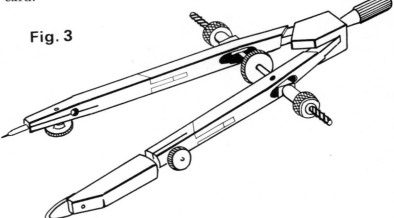

Circular and oval mounts are much easier to cut out of paper or thin card than out of mount board. One either cuts very carefully with a scalpel along a pencilled line drawn with the aid of a template or compass, or directly against a template. Alternatively one can use a compass cutter **(Fig. 3)**. The round-topped paper mounts of the botanical triptych opposite were cut with a compass cutter. It is possible to cut bevelled curved windows out of mount board but it takes a lot of patience, a lot of scoring round and round and deeper and deeper until you have cut right through. Any unevenness can be sanded smooth with flour paper. If the good of your soul is not your main concern . . . art shops occasionally stock ready-cut oval and circular mounts! The type of circular and oval mount cutter used by professional framers is not worth acquiring unless you intend becoming a full-time framer.

Bevelled edges on mount windows are not compulsory, but they do have a less abruptly recessing effect than vertically cut edges. With both the knife and straightedge and mount cutter methods described on page **26** it is possible to vary the angle of the bevel, but between 50° and 60° is the angle to aim for.

Double mounts (hinged mounts with two fronts, each with a window in it) are a way of adding interest to the space between the picture and the frame. *French mounts*, with ink and wash lines around the window, have the same purpose. Both devices are used in the 'Trout' frames on pages **34** and **35**. However, neither the extra window nor the extra lines should compete with the picture for attention. Their purpose is to direct the eye into the picture.

Cutting a second mount front with a window larger than the first, in the same colour board as the first, is almost equivalent to ruling a white line around the first window opening. What one sees from a distance is the white surface of the second bevel. On the other hand a second window can be used to echo a second colour present in the picture. One often sees the first mount window in paper and the second in mount board, which not only reduces mount cutting time but also achieves a two-tone effect without unnecessarily recessing the picture. In the botanical triptych below both mount fronts were cut out of paper, using two tones of green.

Triptych frames, three separate frames hinged together, can be displayed on a desk top as well as the wall

The distance between the first and second mount windows should be fairly small (1.5 cm or less) or the eye tends to stray off into the mount rather than stay inside the window. Ink and wash lines too far away from a window edge entail the same risk. Single or double ink lines should be ruled within 5 to 10 mm of the window edge. Multiple ink lines enclosing a band of wash should occupy a band not wider than about 2.5 to 3 cm, starting 5 to 10 mm from the window edge. The pale brown, blue and red wash lines of differing thicknesses around the 'Trout' on page **34** start 8 mm from the window edge; the faint green band of wash, flanked by these lines, is 1 cm wide.

There are many gorgeous shades of ink sitting in art shops but they have to be liberally diluted with water for the present purpose or they look much too bold and showy. Watercolours used for the wash band have to be massively diluted for the same reason. Having lightly outlined the band in pencil brush the area inside the pencilled lines with water. This helps the board to absorb the colour evenly. While it is still damp carefully apply the colour between the lines with a soft watercolour brush. When the wash is dry the edges of the band are defined with pen lines of the same colour, less diluted. Professional looking wash lines demand a steady hand and a non-spattering pen (a special ruling pen, see Fig. 14a, page **19**, or a good fountain pen) but are well worth the trouble, especially when mounting watercolours and engravings. Before you start make sure the surface of your mount board is suitable for ink and watercolour.

Mounts with multiple windows have a strong visual impact of their own. This is why they are best confined to a subject one is obliged to peer at. From a distance the mount used for the stamps, E on page **36**, makes a bold pattern of rectangles and triangles. To see the stamps properly one has to stand close, and at that distance the pattern of the mount is not really obtrusive.

Fabric-covered mounts tend to be more appropriate for oil paintings (the subject of fabric-covered 'slips' is discussed on page **64**), photographs and three-dimensional subjects than for the genres discussed in this chapter. However, there are occasions when the texture of a fabric enhances a print or drawing. Fabric is rarely used to face single mounts because of the problem of attaching paper to fabric, but no such

Fig. 4

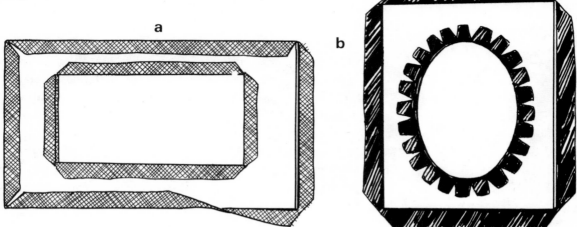

a

b

problem is involved in covering the window half of a hinged mount. The simplest way to do this is to cut a piece of fabric a little larger all round, glue it to the mount front, cut out the middle, then fold and glue the edges to the back of the mount window **(Fig. 4a, b)**. The best adhesive for the job is Spray Mount, sprayed evenly over the entire card surface, including the bevelled edge of the window. Results are most satisfactory with fairly thin fabrics – muslin, lawn, linen, moiré.

Frames

The technicalities of making an ordinary mitred frame have been described in Chapter 2. The colour of the frame, like the colour of the mount, should echo one or more of the colours in the picture. With mouldings that you make up yourself almost any colour can be obtained with judicious staining and painting (Chapter 8).

To really belong to a picture a frame should be kindred in spirit as well as colour. A drawing or etching for example looks infinitely more dignified in a modest box, spoon, cushion or flat moulding than in an ornate gold contraption. The little garden gate etching on page **58** would have been overpowered by anything other than a plain, narrow moulding. To gently stress the cheerfulness and untutored originality of the child's painting on page **70** we made a frame with abutted corners. Despite their rustic appearance abutted corners require a little more craftsmanship than the mitred sort. Their construction is discussed in Chapter 7, pages **87–8**.

If mounts generally get narrower as pictures get larger, the converse is true of frames. As with all generalities though there are exceptions. A small portrait, for instance, gains in presence and intimacy by being framed in a wide moulding. An example of this is the portrait of Edward VI, L on page **71**. Also the darker the dominant tones in a picture the darker the frame can afford to be. Here again Edward VI is a good example. So are the two Nicholsons on page **47**.

Gold frames can easily look brash and pretentious if they are too wide or too florid. Our personal preference is for narrow, plain gold mouldings, or else for mouldings with a narrow band of gold in them or with a gold slip in the rebate. To a lesser degree these remarks apply to silver mouldings too. The gold slip used in portraits F and L on pages **36** and **71** is inserted between the glass and the front of the rebate (**Fig. 5**). Slips are made up just like ordinary mitred frames, with their outside dimensions the same size as the rebate.

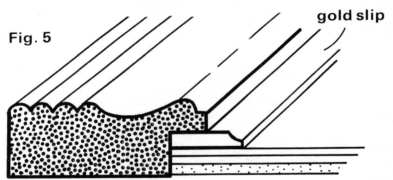

Fig. 5

gold slip

Aluminium frames look best with very colourful modern subjects. Their virtue is their neutrality – they exert next to no favourable or unfavourable influence on their subject. As explained on page **11** metal skin mouldings can be cut with a tenon-saw, but solid metal mouldings are best bought in kit form, unless you are prepared to invest in some sophisticated equipment.

Just occasionally one comes across a picture which strongly resists the enclosing effect of a frame, in which case one has to resort to one of the no-frame options described in Chapter 7. For what it's worth one is always safer going for simplicity than for lots of fussy detail. A simple disaster is less expensive than a complicated one!

Framing watercolours

Watercolour is a wonderfully transparent medium, vivid but delicate. And yet with terrible frequency one sees frail watercolours struggling inside muddy, deadening mounts and dark, fussy frames. What a watercolour really needs is air and light.

On the whole whites, creams, very pale beiges and greens are the colours which are kindest to watercolours. They add light, sometimes subtle warmth as well. Pink and yellow tend to look sickly, blue and grey rather chilly. Dark colours are generally less successful, because more severe, but their formality can be enlivened with a white wash line or two.

If one tries different tones of the same colour against a particular painting it immediately becomes obvious which is kindest to it. Invariably you'll find that the one you like best is one which picks up, probably in a slightly lighter or darker tone, a colour which is in the painting, and probably not the most dominant or the most dramatic one. Generally it is a mistake to attempt to match exactly the colour of a background because this makes it difficult to see where the painting ends and the mount begins. It is really not the role of a mount to be mistaken for part of the painting.

Some watercolours go right to the edge of the paper they are painted on. One can either tip them on to their backing so that the entire paint surface is visible, or obscure part of it under the edge of a mount window. A good compromise is to make the mount window large enough to show a small area of the backing all round the painting. Even when the painting stops well short of the edges of the paper, don't trim it down to sight size, especially if it doesn't belong to you.

French mounts, mounts decorated with ink or wash lines, are particularly suited to watercolours, with the provisos mentioned on page 51.

Dark frames are not especially kind to watercolours. Infinitely preferable are mouldings in the light or mid-brown range, or with plenty of white in them.

Framing prints

The word 'print' covers a multitude of reproductive techniques. The distinction between a print and a reproduction is one of quality and quantity really. Prints are 'multiple originals', executed, or at least supervised in their execution, by the artist himself and produced in limited numbers. Reproductions on the other hand are not necessarily the same size as the original, nor are they produced by the same means, and they certainly aren't propagated in small numbers. Engravings, discussed separately because their fine line and special tonal qualities require special consideration, can belong to either category.

Genuine prints produced by methods other than engraving, that is woodcuts, silk screen prints, lithographs, etc., have considerable value and deserve the protection of glass. Naturally the entire print area should be left visible, and also any state number or artist's signature. The general remarks about mount and frame proportions made earlier in this chapter apply as much to prints as to watercolours or drawings. Prints are so varied in their visual impact that it is impossible to generalize about their treatment, except to say that very bright, bold colours look best against white or cream and stand up well to simple coloured frames (painted or stained as described in Chapter 8). They may also be suitable candidates for an aluminium frame or one of the no-frame treatments discussed in Chapter 7.

Framing engravings and drawings

Restraint is really the key to framing most monochromatic subjects, whether it is their graphic or tonal qualities which predominate. This applies as much to drawings (pencil, ink, crayon, charcoal, gouache, pastel) as to the whole tribe of prints (line engravings, stipple or crayon engravings, mezzotints, aquatints and etchings).

If sepias and browns are the dominant tints beware of colourful frames and mounts. They distract attention and 'kill' the subtle tones of the subject. On the other hand a mount faced with a neutral colour – cream, white, any one of a number of sandy colours, beiges, quiet browns – has the effect of enlivening the subject and keeping the attention where it belongs, on the subject. Grey or sepia wash lines on the mount are sometimes very flattering to a sepia subject.

Where blacks or greys predominate one can add a hint of colour in the mount or frame. Here again though fairly neutral mount tones – white, cream, sandy colours, pale greys, possibly dark greens and dark browns – work best.

If the sobriety of a neutral mount and monochrome subject is a little depressing choose a moulding that has a tasteful gold line in it. It will add just the note of luxury and liveliness you are probably looking for. The Hogarth frames one still sees around so many engravings were evolved when the fashion was for adornment rather than modest enhancement. Apart from the fact that Hogarth-type mouldings are fairly commonly available there is little to recommend them. To our mind they have a rather fussy feel to them.

Another way of adding non-destructive interest to a neutral mount would be to add a second mount window, in a slightly darker tone than the first, or make the first window white and keep your neutral colour for the second.

Coloured drawings and prints have some of the qualities of watercolours and so react well to most watercolour treatments. However, they stand up rather better to darker mounts and frames than watercolours do.

There are two special considerations concerning the 'sight area' of engravings. First it is an unwritten rule that the 'plate mark' should be visible all round the engraving, and second that the written information underneath the engraving should be left showing. With the ordinary run of older engravings there is usually some spidery lettering (title of the engraving, name of the artist and engraver, date and place of publication) engraved underneath the picture but inside the plate mark. On some engravings, however, this information appears outside the plate mark. The little etching on page **58** illustrates both principles: the plate mark shows through the window, and the window has been cut large enough to show the print number and artist's signature at the bottom. Incidentally the plate area of old prints can be cleaned by gently rubbing finely crumbled art gum rubber (a cheese grater is extraordinarily useful here) over it; this is less abrasive than using art gum in a block and also more effective at picking up the dirt.

'Garden Gate' by Mary Bridger, etching 14 × 12 cm. A narrow box moulding, waxed, and a plain mount faced with heavy textured white cartridge are all that this corner of a cottage Eden needs. A smaller or darker mount would have been rather claustrophobic. As it is there is plenty of space between the window edges and the plate mark.

Original drawings are not always symmetrically positioned on the paper but they can be so positioned inside a mount opening. Once again it is not 'done' to trim a drawing to the desired sight size as it is likely to destroy much of its value. This applies to original subjects in all genres and to limited editions as well.

CHAPTER 4

Oils and acrylics

Framing options for oils and acrylic paintings are rather
greater than for prints and watercolours. This is because they
are frequently more robust in spirit and do not usually
require glazing. This is not to imply that any painting can be
happily pushed into any sort of frame, far from it, or that
there are not cases for glazing. Glass does give some small
paintings a pleasing precious quality. Giving an oil painting
in particular the right sort of frame can involve some taxing
decisions. Several factors may influence your final verdict,
not least the cost of the moulding, which can rise pretty
dramatically if the painting is large. You may need to
consider too where the painting will hang. Will it fit in with
its surroundings, will it clash with a companion painting? If
it is destined for a gallery you may need to take account of
the style of framing which that gallery prefers. If you have
none of these difficulties to contend with you are fortunate.
Even so, guiding principles are not easy to formulate in an
area that basically boils down to a matter of taste. However,
in discussing four different framing methods, we trust that
certain reasons for their use will emerge, so that though the
right answer for your particular problem may not immediately spring to mind you will at least be able to cogitate
more constructively on the viable alternatives.

One precept worth mentioning though is that very small
paintings benefit from a really wide recessed frame. This
tends to draw the eye into the picture and provides an
agreeable air of intimacy. Larger paintings can take either a
wide or a narrow frame. The onus is on you the framer to
give each subject a frame that harmonizes with it, provides
the appropriate atmosphere and doesn't shout louder than
the painting itself. Having said all that, it is ultimately a
matter of personal taste and there's no pleasing all of the
people all of the time.

These days many people paint on prepared boards, usually a tough, unbendable fibre board with a canvas surface texture. These present no framing problems. However, many artists prefer to paint on canvas stretched over a wooden frame or stretcher. These are designed to be adjustable so that if the canvas becomes a little slack it can be tightened by tapping in the wedges in the corners of the wooden frame. Small discrepancies in squareness can be disguised in the framing.

Simple batten-edge frame

This is by far the cheapest method of framing a large oil or acrylic and leaves the whole paint area visible. Have a look at the example shown on page 70, colour illustration K. This is a large acrylic painting, almost an abstract, with crisp, clear lines and fresh, bold colours. It hardly demands a frame at all, certainly nothing fussy, just one that finishes and unobtrusively defines the edges. So we used a 12-mm-thick pine batten sealed with French polish and waxed.

This particular acrylic was done on a sheet of hardboard supported at the back by a 15-mm-square wooden batten glued and pinned to the edges, so we merely glued and pinned the 12-mm batten round these edges to make the frame. **Fig. 1** shows a cross-section of this arrangement. Notice that the front edge of the batten is proud (by about 3 to 5 mm) of the surface of the painting. This protects the painting and tends to disguise any irregularities in the edges of it. Brown gum strip over the back of the two battens blocks any chinks of daylight that may be visible from the front of the frame. If you are framing a painting board add battens around the back edges of it, fixed in place with small brass pins tapped through from the front of the board. The pins will be virtually invisible anyway but painting over the heads will totally disguise them. Make sure the pins are brass as ordinary steel rusts after a while.

If the painting is truly square, make up a mitred batten frame to fit it exactly, then push the painting into it and pin. If it is a little out of square you are better off abutting the battens around it as shown in **Fig. 2a** or **b**.

You may prefer a 'metal look' frame instead. In this case

Fig. 1

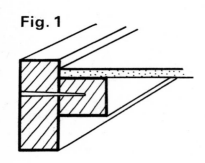

Fig. 2

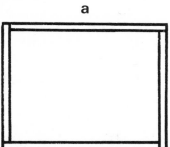
a

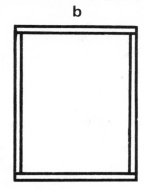
b

Fig. 3

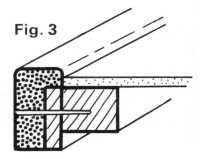

buy a flat section, 'metal look' canvas moulding (proper canvas mouldings have a fairly deep rebate), glue in a length of batten to fill the rebate **(Fig. 3)** and treat as above.

Paintings on canvas stretchers are candidates for the batten-edge treatment too, provided the canvas folds at the corners of the stretcher are not too bulky. Just pin the frame directly to the wooden stretcher **(Fig. 4)**.

Fig. 4

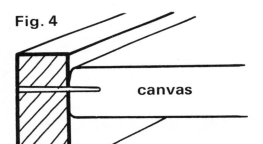
canvas

Fig. 5

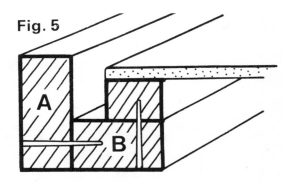
A

B

Floating frame

This is a simple but very versatile type of frame, again using plain pine (or hardwood) batten rather than a ready-finished picture moulding. It suits all sorts of modern paintings very well. Look at the example on page **62**. This acrylic painting has a large area of white in it and needs to retain its feeling of airiness and space. Any frame which hugs the edge would be stifling, but a floating frame answers perfectly. This treatment can be used for paintings on a canvas stretcher or one on a thin board reinforced by batten glued and pinned to the back edges (as in Fig. 1, page **60**). There are two ways of putting a floating frame together.

1   Use two pieces of batten, A and B, and glue and pin them together as in **Fig. 5**. Mitre this 'moulding' as usual and make up a frame calculated to leave a gap between the

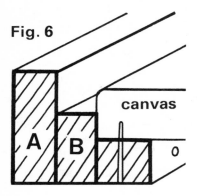

Fig. 6

canvas

A   B   0

'Barns' by Lorna Arnott, acrylic on hardboard, 50 × 75 cm. An example of a floating frame, a simple and effective setting for modern oils and acrylics. The floating effect is achieved by staining or painting the recess around the picture a darker colour than the rest of the frame. Two rectangular sections of pine were used to make this particular frame.

edge of the canvas and batten A. Centre the canvas in the frame and secure by screwing into the wooden stretcher (or batten) through B.

2   Use two battens, A and B, glued and pinned together as in **Fig. 6**. Then make up a frame such that the canvas just fits snugly inside B. To hold the painting in the frame glue and pin four pieces of batten to the inside of B, creating a ledge for the canvas to sit on. Arrange this so that the face of the canvas is a little lower than the top edge of A. Screw through the battens into the wooden stretcher.

Before you finally fix the painting in its frame, decide what finish the frame should have. You could leave it natural with a wax finish, stain it, or paint it to echo a colour in the painting (see Chapter 8 on waxing, staining and painting). The important thing is that the recess should appear dark to strengthen the illusion that the painting is 'floating' in its frame. So, paint the inside edge of A and the top of B in a dark colour, preferably matt. The edge of the painting left visible can be covered with a strip of dark tape just to complete the

moated effect. Cover the back joins in the moulding with brown gum strip to ensure that no daylight is visible through the frame.

Platform frame

Sometimes a painting requires something other than a frame to set it off. The little oil on page 70, colour illustration I, doesn't ask for the intimacy that a wide frame might provide, yet it would lose significance in a narrow one. It needs to stand alone and uncluttered and the platform treatment is an appropriate solution that allows the paint surface to be thrust forward and gain importance.

Fig. 7

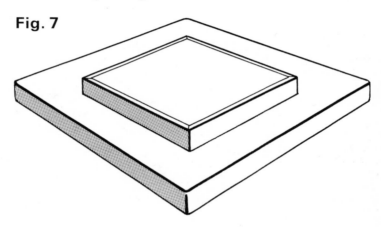

The platform treatment works best when you create a visible stepped effect – one block on top of another **(Fig. 7)**. The small oil in question was in fact painted on paper, so this was mounted on hardboard and then on a piece of chipboard. The edges of this 'picture block' were finished with a very thin (about 3 mm thick) piece of mitred ramin batten painted white. The picture block was then screwed to a backing block of chipboard which had been plastered with filler and painted to give a rough whitewash finish in keeping with the subject.

The backing block could be made from pine, plywood or chipboard left as plain wood, stained or painted, or covered with fabric. In the platform treatment used on page 72 the backing board is covered with cork wall tiles and the edges finished with a thin wooden lipping painted black.

You'll find more about platform frames on page 85.

Rebated frames and slips

Certain subjects, especially those of an impressionistic or delicate nature, look quite out of place in the sort of plain, angular frames we've just been talking about. They often require a more subtle transition between painting and frame. This may be achieved by having a frame with a certain amount of interest in the moulding, that is one with a certain period feel, or by having a combination of frame and slip. Small paintings in particular can look very comfy in the more complicated arrangement of outer frame, wide slip and inner frame.

It is possible to buy special canvas mouldings which have an extra-deep rebate made to accommodate the thickness of a canvas stretcher. You can also buy slips. Two sorts commonly available are the small, flat, gold type (No. 33 on page **33**) and a wide thick one with a sloping face covered with linen (No. 34 on page **33**). This second sort may have its own rebate. A third option is to make up your own fabric-covered slip. This is exactly the same as making a fabric-covered mount (see page **52**), except that you can use much thicker cardboard. We made up a linen-covered slip for the oil painting shown on page **69**, colour illustration H. A delicate green liner was chosen to pick up the predominant tone in the painting and a fraction of gold slip showing inside the linen slip modestly starts the transition from painting to frame. The simple wooden frame, echoing the darker flower tones, does nothing to disrupt this picture's atmosphere of peace and tranquillity.

How does one juggle with a frame, slip and thick canvas and fit them all together? The simplest combination of course is a canvas stretcher (or a painting board) pinned into a canvas moulding **(Fig. 8)**. However, you may want to put a stretcher into a moulding with a shallow rebate. In this case pin some small wooden blocks to the back of the frame and secure the canvas against these with turnclips **(Fig. 9)**. If the canvas is only a little bit proud of the rebate you could pin into the back of the frame and turn the heads of the pins over the edge of the canvas **(Fig. 10)**.

Fig. 8

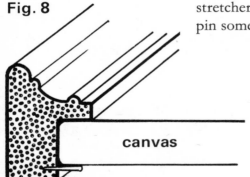

canvas

Fig. 9

canvas

turnclip

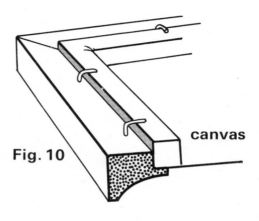

Fig. 10

canvas

Perhaps, on the other hand, you want to use a thin gold slip to make the break between painting and frame and also prefer not to lose any of the paint area. In this case pin some wooden batten round the edge of the canvas stretcher, fit it into the frame and secure by pinning through the side of the frame into the batten in a few places **(Fig. 11)**. Drill pilot holes through the moulding first. Recess the heads of the pins, fill the holes and touch them up.

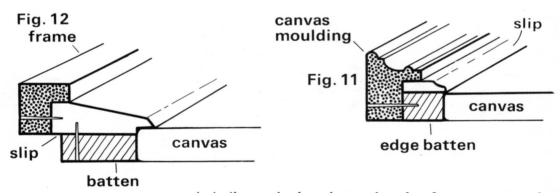

Fig. 12
frame

slip

canvas

batten

canvas
moulding

slip

Fig. 11

canvas

edge batten

A similar method can be employed to fix a canvas stretcher to a thick bevelled slip **(Fig. 12)**. Make sure the slip is securely pinned into the frame first. Note that the batten need only be short lengths on each side of the canvas, or neater still it can be reduced to four mitred corners. The principle is the same – the batten corners simply bridge the gap between the canvas edge and a firm fixing point on the frame.

Take for instance the oil painting on page **69**. This has an outer frame made up from two pine sections. We then made a fabric-covered slip about 6 cm wide. A narrow gold slip was then glued with Bostik to the edge of this fabric-covered

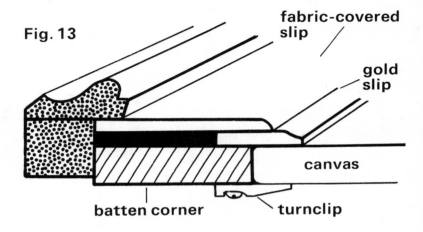

Fig. 13

fabric-covered slip

gold slip

canvas

batten corner

turnclip

slip. To fix the whole assemblage together we made up four wooden corners. These were glued into the corners of the frame and a sliver of cardboard (shaded black in **Fig. 13**) used to fill the gap created by the gold slip. The canvas was held into these corners by turnclips. **Fig. 14** will give you a clearer idea of the whole arrangement.

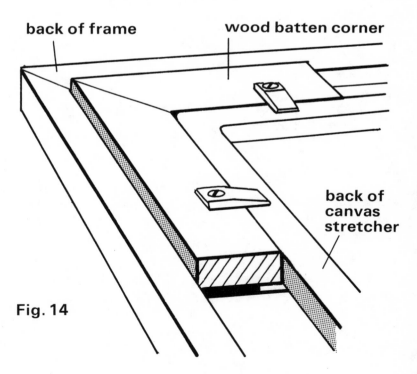

back of frame

wood batten corner

back of canvas stretcher

Fig. 14

If all this seems a bit complicated, don't worry; it's much harder to write (and read) about it than to actually do it. Never mind if your canvas or the fixing battens/corners stand proud of the back of the frame. So long as they are a centimetre or two in from the very edge of the frame they will not be visible when the picture is hung. The edges of the frame will simply stand a little away from the wall and that is no crime.

The possible permutations, given various combinations of frame and slip which themselves vary in width and thickness, are immense. We can't provide a diagram for every contingency but it's rarely difficult to work out a solution along the lines of the examples we've given here. It helps greatly to draw out a cross-section of the arrangement you want to use.

CHAPTER 5

Photographs and posters

As subjects for framing, photographs and posters are exceptionally rewarding. Perhaps this is because they offer such obvious clues to place, time and mood. Essentially one has two alternatives, to stress their period flavour or go for something very simple and modern.

The older the photograph or poster concerned the less inclined one is to materially affect it in any way, as one certainly does by the block mounting methods described below. Glass being the safest method of protecting printed and painted surfaces, the traditional glazed frame (Chapter 2) and the glass and clips type frame (Chapter 7) are the methods which naturally commend themselves.

Photographs and posters which are predominantly black and white or sepia merit the same restraint in their framing as engravings. In other words the window they are seen through or the background they are displayed against should be neutral in tone (white, ivory, beige, brown, grey, dark brown, black). With coloured subjects one can start to pick up colour details, cautiously in the case of delicate subjects, more boldly if the subject is a very vivid one. As mentioned before, white is tremendously effective with bright colours. Even so, though one can never go disastrously 'wrong' with white as a setting, it is most effective at the monochromatic and full technicolour ends of the spectrum. With delicately coloured subjects there is usually a more pleasing solution than white. In this middle range one is looking for unobtrusive flattery rather than contrast.

A word about the paper size of posters. Since they are designed to be displayed just as they are, most posters already have an appropriate width of border around them. There is little point in trying to make a poster look like anything else, so avoid masking any part of the print surface and if possible leave the borders showing. 'Tipping on' is the

H 'Jug of Flowers' by Morris Nitsun, oil on canvas, 75 × 50 cm. With a subject as fresh and delicate as this the transition between the picture area and the frame is particularly important. The pale green linen-covered mount with its gold lip confines the painting without stifling it, at the same time adding a hint of texture and richness. The fairly robust rosy-brown frame was made from two sections of DIY pine moulding, stained and waxed.

H

I 'Houses' by Morris Nitsun, oil on paper, 17 × 17 cm. The last thing this vibrant little oil needed was an enclosing frame. Paintings particularly strong on 'presence' benefit from the kind of platform treatment shown here and described in detail on page **63**.

J Poster painting by Tracy Jackling (age 6), poster paints on sugar paper, 56 × 40 cm. An example of an abutted frame (made from two rectangular sections of pine stained and varnished) complementing a lack of contrivance and a great zest for colour. The poster colours are so exuberant that yellow, a colour with great spiritual energy, seemed the inescapable choice for the mount.

K 'Dunes' by Lorna Arnott, acrylic on hardboard, 90 × 120 cm. The simple batten edging which 'frames' this painting is purely functional, to prevent damage to the edges. As a general rule the larger the painting and the fewer the figurative references it contains the less need it has of an obvious frame. It cannot help attracting attention by virtue of its size and strangeness. The wall against which it hangs is frame enough.

J

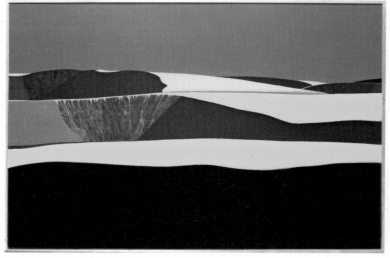

K

M 'A Woman', attributed to Robert Campin (1378–1444), reproduction, 35 × 25 cm. This is an example of a 'tramline' frame, a type of frame common in Campin's day when frames were still an integral part of paintings. Here the tramline is decorated with different wood veneers. The mouldings used for the outer and inner frame were bought in their raw state and stained to match one of the brown tones in the portrait. The construction of tramline frames is discussed on page **87**.

M

L Edward VI after Hans Holbein (1497/8–1543), postcard reproduction. Wide, deeply recessing frames are a classic method of creating an intimate setting for small subjects such as still-lifes and portraits. Far from overpowering the subject a wide dark frame creates a sense of intense inner life. The moulding used here is the same as that used around the 'Trout', **D** on page **35**, but stained black. The gold slip emphasizes the exalted rank of the sitter.

N Military medals, Second World War. This frame opens so that the other side of the medals can be examined. Coloured ribbons look brightest on a neutral ground, in this case deep-pile grey velvet. The orangey richness of the frame, a ready-finished moulding with a maple veneer, echoes this brightness without detracting from it. Medals look more formal and impressive in rows of course than in other patterns. The three-stage construction of this type of frame is described on page **78**.

N

O Needlepoint sampler by Sally Geeve, 18 × 23 cm. The colour, texture and general cosiness of this subject provided a good excuse for a generously curved painted frame and a linen-covered mount. The unworked edges of the sampler, hidden by the mount, were stapled to the mount back.

O

P Three flower illustrations, 20 × 16 cm, by Margaret Stones, Kew Gardens calendar. 'Triptych' frames like this are ideal vehicles for sets of things. In this instance the modest impact of the botanical drawings is reinforced by the triptych treatment and by the arched windows in the paper mounts.

P

Q Weave by Livia Edelstein, satin ribbon, 30 × 25 cm. This box-type showcase was designed to focus as much attention as possible on the special qualities of the weave and protect it from dust and dirt. It had to be glazed, it had to be deep (about 5 cm) and it had to be very simple. White proved to be the best foil to the pinks and greys in the weave, but an all white frame would have been deadening, hence the silver gilt front, which picks up some of the metallic quality of the greys in the weave.

Q

R 'Sheep in Strand', London Transport photograph, enlarged to 37 × 51 cm. This photograph was wet-mounted on a chipboard platform, with smooth, painted edges, and backed with another piece of chipboard covered in cork and edged with black painted batten. Neutral backgrounds are generally more successful with monochromatic subjects than noticeably coloured ones.

R

solution that most naturally comes to mind. In a subtle way the attention-seeking character of a poster is weakened by putting it behind a mount window.

Photographs on the other hand look just as good trimmed to the desired sight area as masked by a mount window. However, it would be a pity to trim an old photograph, denying posterity the pleasure of a gilt edge or an intriguing inscription like 'Aggie and friend at Eastbourne, 1902'. If the information on the back of a photograph, or any other picture for that matter, is particularly interesting a double-sided frame (described on pages **88–9**) might be the answer.

Portrait photographs lend themselves to unusual mounts. Fabrics (moiré silk, damask, cotton, prints, lace, gingham, satin, velvet) and papers (marbled papers, old letters, newspaper cuttings) which look positively vulgar with other subjects look perfect around portraits provided they say something about the period or personality of the sitter. The pale green moiré silk around the sepia portrait on page **36**, colour illustration F, echoes something of the formality and dash of the Edwardian era.

Block mounting

Crudely speaking block mounting involves glueing a subject, trimmed to the desired size, to a thick board (plywood or chipboard for example) cut to the same size or slightly bigger. Refining the concept, the edges of the board can be smoothed, bevelled and sealed with paint or varnish, or finished with a batten of stained or painted wood, or the board can be attached to a second, larger board, painted or covered in fabric, cork, cane or tiles and edged with more batten, and so on and so on . . .

Block mounting is essentially a platform treatment (also discussed in Chapter 7) in which the subject goes out to meet the viewer instead of retiring into a shallow recess. A lot of Old Master reproductions are sold today in ready-to-hang, block-mounted form, usually to their detriment. True, such reproductions are a pale reflection of the originals but they deserve more sympathetic treatment. For low-cost reproductions of engravings, modern prints or abstract paintings, however, block mounting is a cheap and simple solution.

There is a wet method and a dry method of block mounting, the wet involving the use of glue of some kind and the dry the use of special dry mounting film. In either case the mounting board has to be cut to size first, and the edges filled and smoothed before being varnished or painted (not necessary if they are to be hidden with a wooden batten). There are several types of board suitable for block mounting: high-density chipboard, which has a very hard, smooth surface; plywood at least 1 cm thick; 6-mm-thick hardboard, with batten screwed to the back to prevent warping and a deepish moulding with a small lip to hide the edges; blockboard, which also has to have a batten to hide the edges; or ply-faced Conti board, also edged with batten.

The glue to use for attaching the subject to the board is Spray Mount (for thin paper) or Photo Mount (for thicker and photographic papers), both of which come in aerosol form; or wallpaper paste (size), mixed to the consistency recommended on the packet. There is no risk that either of the sprays, not being water-based, will cause the mounting board to warp, and they are much easier to use than wallpaper paste. Because it is mixed with water, wallpaper paste is not suitable for mounting subjects which are printed in water-soluble inks.

Wallpaper paste applied to blockboard or plywood or ply-faced Conti board causes warping unless one takes precautions. Chipboard has little tendency to warp and with 6-mm hardboard the tendency can be counteracted by screwing thick batten all around the back edges as already shown in Fig. 1 on page **60**. However, whatever the type of board you use, the surface to which the subject is to be attached must be 'pre-sized'. This means applying a coat of size to the board and letting it dry before you paste the subject on to it. It is the wetting of only one side of blockboard, plywood or Conti board which causes warping, so when you apply the pre-size coat wet the reverse of the board as well. Size the back of the poster or photograph and lay it down on the dry pre-sized surface, pressing it down all over with a damp cloth, working methodically from top to bottom or from the centre outwards. Because the surface of the board has received a second wetting, the reverse should be wetted again to prevent warping. To ensure good adhesion while drying, weight everything down with lots of books or telephone directories.

On the whole the chances of the subject deteriorating due to the lack of any surface protection or to the use of any one of several home sealing treatments are about equal. Unfortunately transparent plastic films and varnishes (the sort used to seal oils and acrylics) tend to discolour after a time.

Dry mounting is normally done using a special heat press, but it can be done DIY style, using an ordinary domestic iron to apply the necessary heat and pressure. On the whole though it is not very successful except with very small posters and photographs. Dry mounting film can be bought in most commercial art stores. Lay the subject face down on a clean surface and cover the back with dry mounting film. Touch the centre with the tip of a hot iron so that the film adheres to the subject, then trim the film to the exact size of the subject. Place the subject on its backing (preferably thick cardboard) and iron the surface, protected by a piece of paper, with a hot iron (its setting for linen). This causes the mounting film to melt and bond paper and board together. That said, it is well worth having medium and large subjects commercially dry mounted and laminated. Most large photographic laboratories offer this service.

For subjects which are of more than passing value or cannot easily be replaced, block mounting is a form of vandalism, partly redeemable by putting the subject, block mount and all, behind glass, which would have been the most sensible solution in the first place. In most cases, therefore, it is better not to block mount a subject which you intend, eventually, to frame properly.

CHAPTER 6

Three-dimensional subjects

Some of the most rewarding and challenging subjects to frame are things like coins, medals and insignia, plant materials, fans, collages, samples of weaving, and especially collections of small objects – anything from matchboxes, shells and butterflies to small tins, fishing flies and old buttons. Working out the optimum display arrangement, choosing an appropriate background on which to mount them and finding a way of securing them safely and unobtrusively to that background is as much a part of the framing operation as actually constructing the frame. But one thing all these objects require is a deep frame in which the glass is held away from the objects themselves. Below we discuss three ways of making up a 'showcase' frame of this sort; two are sealed just like an ordinary frame and one is a hinged frame that opens.

Deep-sided box frame

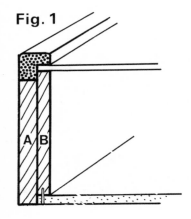

Fig. 1

We used this kind of frame to display a chunky piece of ribbon weaving (see page **72**, colour illustration Q) which was set off to best advantage in a clean-looking, non-fussy frame in silver and white.

The general costruction of the frame is shown in **Fig. 1**. First glue together two pieces of thinnish ramin batten (A and B in Fig. 1). Mitre the lengths and join them to make the sides of the box. Paint or stain the box at this stage. Mount the subject on its base board (see page **78**) and pin into the box. Then use a plain rebated picture moulding to make a frame that neatly fits the top of the box. Place the glass in position and, using a clear adhesive like Bostik or Uhu, glue this top frame in place and weight it down well until the 'hesive is set.

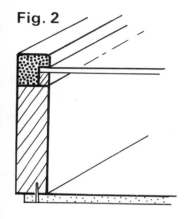

Fig. 2

One can of course make up this box in other ways, for instance using one piece of wooden batten for the box sides and filling the rebate of the top frame with a small wooden strip **(Fig. 2)**. Wood strip of this sort is usually to be found in model-making shops.

Box frames like this one are sometimes used to preserve particularly fragile paintings on wood, bark, ivory, etc.

Shallow display frame

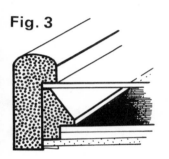

Fig. 3

This showcase requires two rebated picture mouldings – a canvas moulding (i.e. one with a deep rebate) for the outer frame, and a bevelled box moulding for the inner frame **(Fig. 3)**. Make up two ordinary mitred frames, the box one fitting snugly inside the other. Insert the glass, then fix the two frames together by pinning through the rebate of the inner frame into the rebate of the outer one. (Drill pilot holes in the inner frame first.) Finally fix in the base board and add a back board if necessary.

Detail of the showcase frame shown in colour on page **71**. Note the side clips and the deepish box type moulding (sloping profile) used for the inner half of the back frame.

Hinged display case

A frame that opens is sometimes desirable. It is advantageous for example to be able to change or replace specimens in it easily and examine the objects on display more closely –

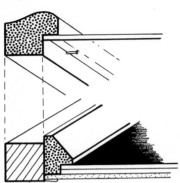

Fig. 4

coins, for instance, have equally interesting obverse sides. You'll need a couple of extras for this kind of case, namely two brass clips to hold the frame closed (see photograph on page 77), and a pair of brass cabinet hinges.

The three-frame construction used for the hinged case shown on page 71 is illustrated in **Fig. 4**. You require an ordinary rebated picture moulding to make the front frame. For the two back frames you need some wooden batten (stained and polished to match the front frame) and some rebated box moulding (No. 22 on page 33).

First make up the front frame. Then construct a frame from the wooden batten so that its outer dimensions are exactly the same as those of the front frame. Next use the box moulding to put together a frame that fits comfortably inside the batten frame. Paint the box frame a colour to tone with the base board (or cover it with matching fabric) and pin it to the batten frame through the rebate.

Hinge the front frame and the back batten frame together. The neatest method is to chisel out recesses for the leaves of the hinges (a long frame like the one we made is best hinged at the top rather than the side). Pin in the base board complete with all display items firmly attached (see below). Then pin in a back board and gingerly pin the glass into the front frame.

Mounting three-dimensional subjects on a base board

All subjects will need to be mounted on some sort of base board, not to be confused with the back board which merely finishes off the back of the frame. This base board could be cardboard or hardboard covered with paper or fabric. Dark velvets have a plushness and formality that set off the bright metal of coins, insignia and jewellery particularly well. Linen and hessian in retiring colours make excellent, textured backgrounds for just about any subject. The wrong side of hardboard – the pitted side – painted an appropriate shade with emulsion paint also makes a useful background.

Attaching medals that have ribbons to a base board is straightforward. Cut slits in the base board (through fabric and all) then push the end of each ribbon through and secure it to the back with sticky tape. Velvet won't fray visibly if it has been glued to the base board all over. Decorations and insignia that have lapel pins on the back of them can be anchored quite adequately by pressing the pins firmly into slits made in the base board. If neither of these methods look as if they'll work for your particular collection, you may have to consider sewing the various pieces to the back board or using small pins to support them.

Coins are a little problematical. The most satisfactory method is to have them sit in recesses in the base board. This means cutting holes in the base board before you cover it with fabric. These holes need to be a trifle larger than the coins themselves so that each coin is a good press fit when the edge of its hole is covered in fabric. Cutting holes in a cardboard base board is a bit laborious but not difficult. Making them in hardboard would require the aid of a mechanical circle cutter (one of the attachments you can buy for a power drill). Place each coin in position on the base board and draw round it in pencil. Use a scalpel or a craft knife to score round and round until you get through, then sand the edges of the hole well with flour paper. Make all the holes then cover the board with fabric, snipping small Vs in the material so you can ease the resulting flaps neatly round the edge of each hole and glue them to the back of the board. (Fig. 4b, page **53**, gives you the general idea.) Now cover another board with fabric and use it to back the 'holed' board. This gives the coins something to bed into and creates a finished appearance even when the coins are removed. If all your coins happen to be the same size you could cut down on the work by fitting them into a long oblong recess rather than individual holes. Matchboxes could be candidates for this treatment too.

Mounting a sample of embroidery or weaving is usually no problem. The simplest option is to use some tiny pins to pin it out on a thick cardboard or a fibreboard base. Alternatively, stitch it to the fabric covering the base board or take the stitches right through the base board.

However, samples of this sort often look very much better if they are 'presented', that is stand proud of the base board instead of lying completely flat against it. An effective way of doing this is to stick Velcro strips to the top and bottom of the sample and glue two more strips to a couple of small pieces of wooden batten. The battens are then glued and pinned to the base board so that the sample can be held evenly stretched between them. This is how the ribbon weaving shown on page **72** was mounted on its base board.

Velcro is pretty useful in other quarters too. Plenty of objects defy stitching, glueing and pinning but can be neatly mounted using tiny pieces of Velcro.

Occasionally a letter, perhaps a document or press cutting, at any rate something on paper, needs to be displayed as part of a collection of exhibits. A good way to show it and one that won't damage it in any way, is to face the paper with a piece of glass cut to exactly the right size. This can be held in place with a tiny pin at each corner if the base board is plywood or thick hardboard. If the base board is cardboard the glass can be secured at the corners by small loops of thin, round elastic **(Fig. 5)**. The ends of the elastic of course go through to the back of the board and are anchored there with sticky tape. We used this method to secure the little certificate shown with the medals on page **71**, colour illustration M.

Plant materials – pressed flowers, ferns, leaves etc. – are usually lightweight and can be glued to a base board. But a better plan, which avoids discoloration and damage, is to stitch the specimens to the base board. A stitch here and there across a stem in a neutral-coloured cotton is unobtrusive and very adequate.

Fig. 5

Compartmented frame for ceramic tiles

Framed tiles look particularly attractive. They can of course be put in a frame made from normal rebated picture moulding but invariably this means you lose the edges of the tiles in the rebate. Since the majority of tiles were designed to

Fig. 6 a

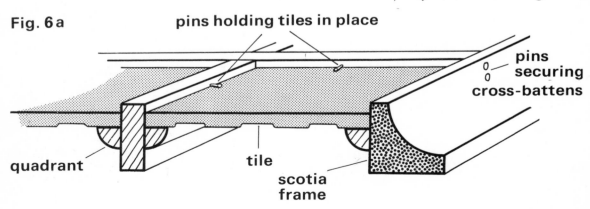

pins holding tiles in place

pins securing cross-battens

quadrant

tile

scotia frame

have their whole surface visible the patterns on many of them go right to the edges, and it can be annoying to have to sacrifice even half a centimetre all round for the sake of a rebate. A neat solution to the problem is shown in the photograph below. Here half a dozen 6-in Victorian tiles are displayed in a compartmented frame made from plain timber mouldings. We made the main frame from pine scotia and used pine batten in two different widths to divide the frame up into its six compartments. Pieces of pine quadrant are pinned to the scotia frame and to the batten divides to create small ledges on which the tiles sit. Little brass pins prevent the tiles from falling out. **Fig. 6a** shows this whole arrangement.

Six Victorian ceramic tiles displayed in a compartmented frame made from DIY pine mouldings stained and waxed. This sort of frame doesn't have a rebate so none of the ceramic surface is obscured

If you go in for collecting single ceramic tiles and have a number to frame, this is an economic way of combining several quite different tiles in one display. A long oblong, 3-compartment frame, or a square 4-compartment layout looks effective too. Scotia used this way round creates a frame in which the tiles are 'presented' rather than recessed, so directing attention to the most important feature, the ceramic surface.

To make a frame of this sort, put together the scotia frame first, taking into account the extra length needed to accommodate the batten divides. Cut the battens roughly to length and where necessary make the joint shown in **Fig. 6b** – make the two 90° cuts in your mitre-box and remove the unwanted tongue of wood with a chisel. Then cut the battens to length so they are a good push fit inside the frame. Secure the ends of the battens with a couple of pins tapped in through the scotia (see Fig. 6a) – drill pilot holes in the scotia first. The frame requires no back and in fact is better off without one so that any identifying marks on the reverse of each tile can be easily seen.

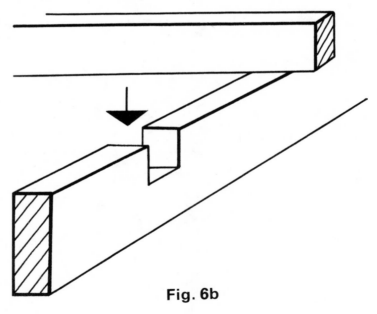

Fig. 6b

CHAPTER 7

No-frame frames, kits and other frames

Specially made frames around works of art are a relatively recent phenomenon. In the Middle Ages paintings were either immovable or done on wooden panels, often with an integral painted border or raised rim. The fashion for separate frames began in the thirteenth century. The framers of the Renaissance, and indeed up until the nineteenth century, were skilled woodcarvers. It was in imitation of the exuberant carved gilt frames of the French Baroque that the Victorians produced their plaster and gilt monstrosities. Today however the emphasis is on simplicity and cleanness of line. So, following the spirit of the age, we will deal with the simplest frames first.

No-frame frames

Block mounting, discussed in the last chapter, constitutes a no-frame method, but it is a fairly temporary, throw-away method of presentation. In terms of the protection it gives, the *glass-and-clip method*, now very popular, is half-way between block mounting and the traditional glazed frame. You simply sandwich the subject, displayed on a single mount or in a hinged mount, between a piece of glass and a piece of hardboard, and use four spring clips (Fig. 15e, page **21**) to hold the assembly together. Perspex (3 mm thick) can be used instead of ordinary picture glass, but it is approximately three times as expensive. Both sides of the glass should be cleaned before assembling. Either make holes in the back board to take the lugs of the spring clips or simply position them and give them a couple of taps with the hammer to secure them. Make sure the whole assembly is lying perfectly flat on the work surface when you do this or you may break the glass.

The finer points of the glass-and-clip method are that all elements (glass, mount, hardboard) should be exactly the same size; that the edges of the glass (or Perspex) should be bevelled or at least smoothed, something the glazier can do if you do not have any wet emery cloth; that you should use bifurcated rivets to attach the D-rings (or a mirror plate) to the hardboard back and hammer the splayed ends of the rivets completely flat; that a hinged mount with a window in it is better protection against dust than a single mount, especially if the mount back is attached to the front with double-sided Sellotape inside all the way round. There is a snag though: large areas of glass, 60 × 90 cm or more, are too heavy to be safely held by spring clips.

Possible alternatives to spring clips in these circumstances are nuts and bolts or mirror corners. Nuts and bolts are structurally stronger than spring clips, because of course they bolt all the elements together, but, unfortunately, ordinary picture glass is too thin for the glazier to drill holes in. So what you gain in strength you lose by being obliged to have thicker glass (4 mm). Perspex is the obvious solution to the weight problem, but an expensive one.

Mirror corners are of two types. With the sort illustrated in **Fig. 1** one needs a backing rather thicker than hardboard, or hardboard plus edge batten, to screw them into. With the other sort **(Fig. 2)** the glass/mount/hardboard sandwich has to be assembled directly against the wall. This is a fairly permanent arrangement, but worth considering if you have a particularly large and therefore heavy piece of glass to support.

Incidentally, if the subject is small and fairly irreverent, glass and hardboard could be held together with brightly painted bulldog clips!

Another no-frame method, a little old-fashioned now, is to stick glass and backing together with *passe-partout*, a gummed tape which comes in various colours. However neat a job one does though, the finished article never has the simple elegance of glass and clips. Again D-rings or mirror plates should be attached to the backing with bifurcated rivets.

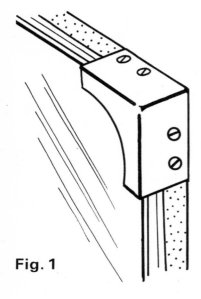

Fig. 1

Fig. 2

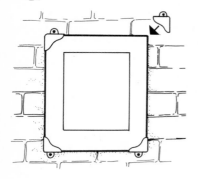

Frame kits

Before we return to frames proper something needs to be said about frame kits. The most commonly available sort are of aluminium, and sold as pairs of sides with the necessary angle plates and screws for joining them. Obviously these are not for anyone seriously interested in acquiring framing skills. Even so, only half the work is done for you, as you still have to cut the glass and backing to size and make a mount. Requiring rather less effort are the sort of kits one buys complete with glass and backing; in this case all four sides, again of aluminium, are supplied together with screws, wire and springs to hold the whole contraption together at the back.

Other frames

There are six examples of non-traditional frames in this book: the two platform frames, one around the small oil on page **70**, the other around photograph R on page **72**; the abutted frame around the child's painting on page **70**; the 'tramline' frame around the Campin reproduction, M on page **71**; the botanical triptych frame on page **72**; and the bamboo frame on page **92**. All of these treatments involve the use of either the 45° or 90° angle of the mitre-box.

The *platform-type frame*, already mentioned in connection with oil paintings and block mounting, is almost opposite in feeling to the traditional frame. It gives a subject a distinct pictorial environment without recessing it or obviously enclosing it. Basically a platform frame is a backing of some kind with the subject displayed on a platform in the middle. The construction of the platform frame around the small oil on page **70** is explained in Chapter 4.

Both the backing and the platform for this sort of frame can be made of blockboard, chipboard, plywood, Conti board, thick hardboard, wood, any material in fact which is, or can be made to look, at least 1 cm thick around the edges and is unlikely to warp. The backing board can be painted or covered to harmonize or contrast with the subject. The photograph on page **72** has a backing board covered with cork wall tiles sealed with polyurethane varnish. Hessian also makes a good covering. Imagination and taste will suggest lots of other covering materials. Any raw edges can be neatened with thin wooden batten, with or without a lip. The batten should be the same depth as the edge it is hiding. The edge of the central platform, if it is unsuitable for painting or staining, will need similar treatment. If you intend to use glass the batten around the central platform will have to have a lip on it to hold the glass in place. **Fig. 3a** and **b** shows a cross-section through a platform frame with and without

Fig. 3

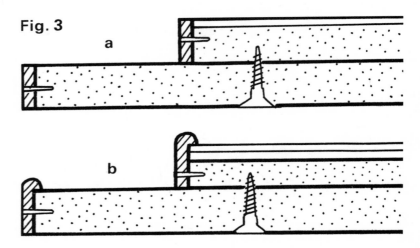

glass. It is best to completely assemble the platform part of the frame before screwing it to the backing. Two screws, screwed through from the back, are quite sufficient.

The *tramline frame* is a close relative of the platform frame anatomically speaking, but its purpose is more frankly decorative. The frame around the Campin portrait, colour illustration M on page **71**, is a tramline frame, with marquetry (wood veneers) in the tramlines. **Fig. 4** shows this type of

Fig. 4

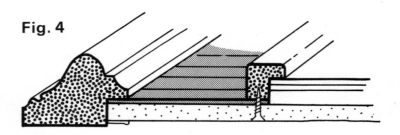

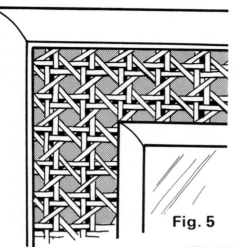

Fig. 5

frame in cross-section. Frames like this are really frames within frames, the outer frame being somewhat wider than the inner. The space between them is decorated in a manner in keeping with the picture. Oriental prints, for example, look particularly attractive with woven cane in the tramlines **(Fig. 5)**. Fabrics with strong textural qualities (brocade, hessian, slub weaves) make good infills too, and ceramic tiles are sometimes used in this way.

Step one is to decide how wide a space you want between the inner and outer frame and then cut a backing board to the rebate size of the outer frame. Next you make and assemble the inner frame as you would any ordinary frame, but omitting the hardboard backing. Next the area between the tramlines is covered with veneer, fabric, cane, etc. Then the outer frame is made up and the backing board slotted into it and pinned in place. Lastly the inner frame is attached to the backing board by pinning through from the back (to do this accurately mark and drill the pin holes from the front). Fig. 4 shows the construction details just described.

Triptych frames (three separate frames hinged together) are uncommon today. Originally they were shallow, ornately carved wooden cupboards used to conceal or reveal icons, relics and other religious subjects. This is why the *volets* or side shutters of Renaissance and earlier triptychs were only half the width of the central panel. The concept deserves updating because it has several natural applications. For example, it is a very logical way of displaying related or sequential subjects: past, present, future; baby, adolescent, adult. All three frames can be the same or different sizes, depending on the nature of the subject. A hinged construction like this gives one the option of hanging it on the wall or standing it on a desk top. The botanical triptych shown on page **72**, colour illustration P, is held together with small brass cabinet hinges.

Abutted frames, such as the one used for the child's painting on page **70**, make a refreshing change from the mitred sort. They add a nice touch to naïve and modern subjects. As you will appreciate after a moment's reflection, proper rebated mouldings pose a problem, as they cannot be abutted to give continuous moulding details on the front. Nevertheless a rebated moulding which has a flat profile with the minimum of detail could be joined as illustrated in **Fig. 6a**. The rebate gaps showing at either end of the two sides are filled with pieces of wooden batten. When making up a frame like this, glue the batten in place first and drill pilot holes for the pins. Then assemble the frame by glueing and pinning.

An abutted frame can also be constructed working with rectangular section timber mouldings. **Fig. 6b** shows how the corners of the frame on page **70** were cut and joined. The

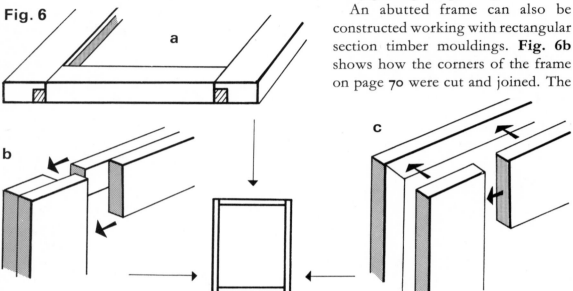

Fig. 6

a

b

c

two mouldings for the sides were glued and pinned before being cut to size. But the two parts of the moulding for the top and bottom were not glued and pinned until the front sections had been cut to size; the rebate extensions were sawn to the correct length later. One alternative to this construction method is to make the rebate part of the frame separately, by the traditional mitre method, and then cut the front pieces and glue and pin them to the rebate, pinning through from the back of course **(Fig. 6c)**.

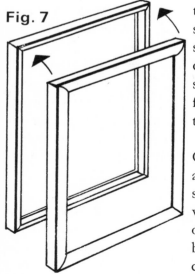

Fig. 7

One rarely comes across *double-sided frames* but their virtues are obvious for subjects with inscriptions on the back or simply to display two subjects at once. For both sides to be visible the frame must stand on a plinth of some kind and obviously the back of the mount must be cut out to show the back of the subject. Whatever construction method you choose, the basic principle is the same: you sandwich two frames together **(Fig. 7)**. One method is to make a mitred frame in the ordinary way, with a rebate deep enough to accommodate the mount and two thicknesses of glass (any excess depth can always be filled with strips of mount board in the rebate) and then make up a second frame of plain or moulded wooden batten and glue it to the back of the first **(Fig. 8a)**. If the front of the frame is made from the same sort of batten as the back, with a rectangular section added between them to make the rebate, there need be no disparity between the back and the front of the frame **(Fig. 8b)**.

Fig. 8

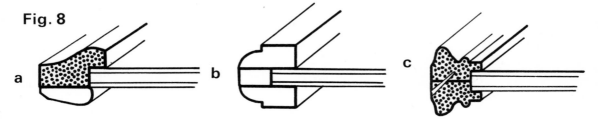

a   b   c

Alternatively you could sandwich two shallow rebated mouldings together **(Fig. 8c)**. In this case it would be advisable to pin as well as glue the join, using one or two long panel pins per side and drilling the holes for them at an angle across the join. The simplest form of plinth is a flat piece of wood with a beading round the edge **(Fig. 9)**. The frame is attached to it by screwing through the base of the plinth.

Fig. 9

The *strut-back frame* is a more common resident of mantelpieces and desk tops than the double-sided sort. Any ordinary frame can be made into a strut-back by attaching a tie-shaped piece of hardboard to the back with a light hinge and a piece of ribbon to prevent the strut opening too far **(Fig. 10)**. Alternatively one can use the clip-on fixing shown in Fig. 15h on page **21**.

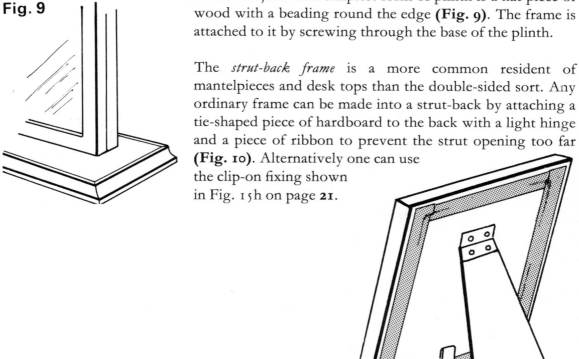

Fig. 10

Round and oval frames have a lot of charm but not all framers today are craftsmen enough to make them. Modern mass-produced rounds and ovals are not difficult to find. With a little staining or spattering (Chapter 8) they can be made to look quite venerable. The subjects traditionally associated with them are portraits, silhouettes, pressed flowers and pieces of needlework. Occasionally though one finds prints and engravings which are round or oval and deserve like frames. The cutting of round and oval mounts is discussed on page 50.

Bamboo frames made of the genuine article rather than the facsimile moulding (No. 16 on page 33) require some ingenuity. First, your bamboo needs to be fairly stout, about 3 cm in diameter. Then, because it is hollow and splits easily, you have to join the corners in a special way. They are first mitred in the usual fashion, after which you make up mitred inserts of wooden dowel **(Fig. 11)** which are more or less a push fit inside the hollow ends of the bamboo. The corners are then pinned as shown in **Fig. 12** and bound with raffia or split cane **(Fig. 13)**.

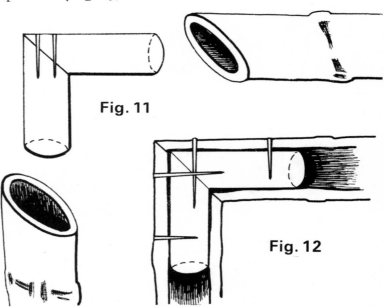

Fig. 11

Fig. 12

To bind the corners, hammer in an anchor pin at the apex of the corner and secure the end of the cane at the back of the frame by starting to loop the free end round the pin as shown in **Fig. 13a**. **Fig. 13b** shows this manoeuvre from the front.

Fig. 13

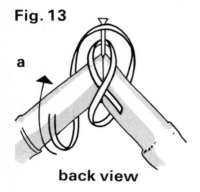

a

back view

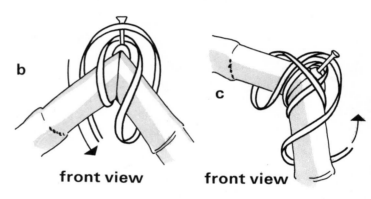

b

front view

c

front view

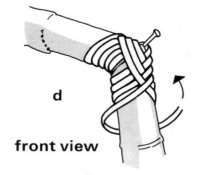

d

front view

Now take the free end alternately around each arm of the frame and alternately around the front and back of the pin (**Fig. 13c**) so that you get a cross-over pattern forming at the sides as shown in **Fig. 13d**, and the photograph overleaf.

The lack of a rebate is solved by pinning pieces of much thinner bamboo, with their ends mitred, to the inside front edge of the frame at frequent intervals **(Fig. 14)**. It may be necessary to cut shallow grooves in the slightly protruding 'joints' of the main frame so that the thin bamboo beading can be pinned flush against it. The back of the picture is also kept in place with thin dowel or bamboo pinned to the main frame (Fig. 14 again).

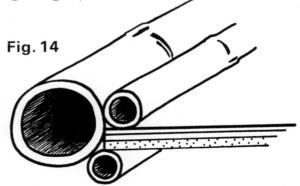

Fig. 14

A very attractive, modern-looking frame can be made on the same principle with ordinary wooden dowel stained red, green, blue, etc.

There are of course many other crafts – embroidery, basketry, caning, leather tooling, plaster moulding, wood-carving, upholstery, various inlay techniques – which can be applied to frame making, but they are incidental to the construction methods discussed here and elsewhere in the book.

A traditional pair, bamboo frame and Oriental subject (a block print on rice paper). The split-cane corner bindings hide the mitred and pinned corners of the frame and also any splitting which may have occured while joining. Bamboo can be colour-varnished but not stained, unless one completely removes its smooth surface.

Close-up of the corner binding of the bamboo frame shown above. The head of the anchor pin, which one hammers in when the binding is finished, can just be seen protruding above the first loops of the binding.

CHAPTER 8

Finishes on frames

A number of ready-finished picture mouldings, mainly oak, ramin and pine, are sold unstained and unpolished, that is 'natural'. Any moulding you make up yourself from pine, ramin or other hardwood will be in the same state. Of course staining, waxing or painting a moulding involves extra effort but it is time well spent if in the end you produce a frame that exactly complements your picture.

Waxing

If you want to leave the moulding natural, sand it well with flour paper (very fine glass paper) and rub on some wax with fine-grade wire wool. A beeswax furniture polish is best, and you can make up your own by mixing equal parts of melted beeswax, pure linseed oil and pure turpentine. Allow the wax to dry and then buff with a soft cloth. Put on a second coat of wax, with a cloth this time, and again rub to a smooth sheen. On beaded or carved mouldings an old soft toothbrush is useful for getting wax into the recesses and a soft clothes brush ideal for buffing.

To provide a more durable surface, give the wood an initial sealing coat of French polish rubbed on with a soft rag. When it is dry apply the wax as before.

Staining

There are several different brands of wood dye or stain. These come in a very good range of wood colours, plus a few brighter colours, and most stains of the same make can be mixed to give in-between shades. Some makes are spirit based, others water based, and they can be diluted with white spirit and water respectively. You can't mix together spirit-and water-based dyes. However, we have found that a spirit-based one does take on top of a water-based one but not vice versa.

Hardwoods stain very well, as their close, regular grain takes up the colour evenly. On the other hand pine, especially the kind from which standard timber mouldings are made, is a little tricky as it absorbs the colour unevenly. This can be remedied to some extent by choosing your wood carefully, by sanding really well prior to staining, cleaning with white spirit, and building up the colour by applying several coats of diluted stain. And of course the colour will tend to even out in time as the pine itself mellows. But to be on the safe side, leave pine natural, give it just a toning-down coat of diluted stain., or take it down to a really dark colour. Whatever the wood you're staining, try the colour out on a scrap piece first.

After staining, give the wood a couple of coats of French polish and then wax. For a really high finish apply several coats of French polish, rubbing down between coats with fine wire wool. French polish is shellac based and gives a very fine smooth finish. It is much preferable to polyurethane varnish and also dries quicker.

Is it better to stain and finish before or after you've made the frame? Well, if you stain a length of moulding before you cut it you can see which parts look best and so cut and match the frame sides accordingly. This is much the best way if you're confident of making a good frame.

What we're going to say now may make a professional framer wince, but it's worth noting all the same as it might make the difference between your producing a frame you can happily live with or chucking it away and starting again. The point is that if you haven't put together a very brilliant frame you can sometimes improve matters by a spot of sanding at the corners just to even them up. Now if the frame has already been stained and polished it's difficult to recolour the sanded parts because the previous finish plus the sanding form a sort of 'resist'. These lighter-coloured patches will just emphasize the corners. Obviously this problem doesn't arise if you stain and finish after you've put the frame together. Even so, a word of warning – be extra careful that you don't get glue on the front surface of the frame, or, if you do, wipe it off immediately, because glue also forms a resist.

Painting

Wooden mouldings that are to be painted should be sanded really smooth first. They can then be treated with grain filler, and this is a good plan if the wood has a slightly coarse grain. When the filler has dried sand it well and put on a coat of wood primer. When this is bone dry sand it with flour paper and apply the first coat of paint. Two or three further coats may be required and it's worth wire-wooling between coats. We find a square-ended, bristle, oil-painting brush is just the job for painting frames. This may all sound a palaver but it's the only way to ensure a good smooth finish.

Gloss paint is fine if you favour a bright, plastic-looking finish. If you want something a bit more subtle use a matt enamel paint (the sort that comes in little tins and is used for model making) and rub down the final coat with fine-grade wire wool. The matt surface will then acquire a beautiful smooth sheen. This was the method used on the red-painted frame shown on page **71**, colour illustration O.

If you want to paint after you've assembled the frame it's best to use a spray paint as this eliminates the possibility of brush marks in the corners. Sand the wood smooth, apply an undercoat and sand again, then apply a couple of coats of spray paint. Spray painting on top of a few coats of well smoothed gesso (see pages **97–8**) will give an excellent finish.

Of all the silver and gold colours around by far the best is the Liquid Leaf range, available from most art shops. We wouldn't recommend that you paint whole frames with it (the resemblance to real gold or silver leaf goes no further than the name), but it is useful for small touching-up jobs. It is equally effective when used to give a plain frame a line of colour, say along the sight edge or on a raised bead. If there is already some gold leaf on the frame the Liquid Leaf will look inferior by comparison, but on its own it's fine. Plain stained wood frames are often enhanced by having a recess or an edge picked out in colour, usually gold or a neutral grey tone, and where possible it is a good idea to mask one or both sides of the line with tape so you get good clean edges **(Fig. 1)**.

Instead of a definite line you may want to add shading, perhaps to give depth to a recess or to echo a tone in the picture. In this case paint along the recess, leave for a few moments then wipe off the excess with a cloth leaving a layer

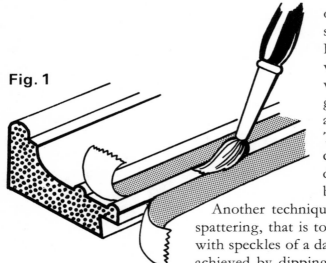

Fig. 1

of colour that shades softly into the surrounding wood. A matt paint like Plaka, which can be thinned with water, works very well. The same 'paint and wipe' principle applies if you want to give a whole frame a sort of bloom by allowing the colour to sit in the grain. To really stress the grain the moulding can be textured first by rubbing in the direction of the grain with a wire brush.

Another technique you may like to experiment with is spattering, that is toning down a gilded or painted surface with speckles of a darkish colour. This effect is very simply achieved by dipping a toothbrush in the colour (oil paint thinned with turpentine), shaking off the excess, then running your finger across the bristles so that flecks of colour, 'flyspecks', are flicked on the surface.

Gilding

Gilding is a profession in its own right but it has traditionally been considered part of a picture framer's art. Many established picture framers still undertake gilding work, but the skill is less called for nowadays than when heavy and richly moulded gilt frames were in vogue. The trend today is towards lightweight, plain gilt mouldings and these are bought ready-gilded from a manufacturer. Metal-skin moulding has also found a place in the market.

There are various sorts of real gold leaf – English, West German, French and Italian are the main ones. These differ in both price and tonal quality. All are wickedly expensive and the price of a little book of it (usually twenty-five $3\frac{1}{4}$-in-square leaves) would buy you a goodly footage of ready-gilded moulding. 'Metal' leaf, also bought in books of slightly larger leaves, is copper based, hence cheaper and widely used to simulate real gold. Then there is 'transfer gold'. This consists of an extremely thin layer of gold laid down on a backing paper. It is applied just like a transfer, that is pressed down on to the gilding surface and the tissue back peeled off.

It must be said that applying gold leaf is a skill that requires considerable practice and one probably best learnt by attending a course or class. But if you do want to dabble you'll find *Practical Woodcarving and Gilding* by W. Wheeler and C. H. Hayward informative. Some art shops keep books of loose leaf gold and the transfer gold but rarely the whole range of gilding materials. The supplier listed in the back of this book keeps everything you're ever likely to need.

There are two basic methods of applying gold leaf – water gilding and oil gilding. The difference between the two in terms of the result obtained is that with water gilding the leaf is burnished to a high shiny finish, whereas in oil gilding it is not burnished at all and so remains matt.

Gilding usually requires four specialist tools – a gilder's cushion **(Fig. 2a)**, tip **(b)**, knife **(c)**, and burnisher **(d)**. The knife is used to separate the delicate leaf and lay it on the cushion where it can be cut and flattened out ready for use.

Fig. 2

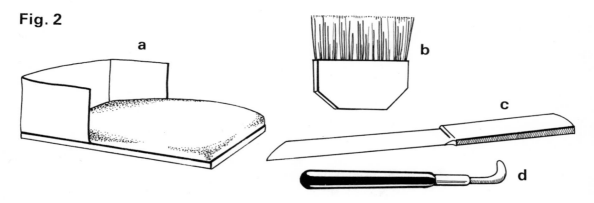

The cushion consists of a small padded board covered with soft suede, and has a protective shield to guard against draughts. The tip is a flat brush made from card and hair which is used to pick up the leaf from the cushion and transfer it to the gilding surface. To make the leaf adhere to the brush, the brush is stroked across the palm of the hand, or the hair, so that it collects a trace of grease – enough to pick up the leaf. The agate-tipped burnisher is used in water gilding to bring a high finish to the leaf once it has been laid.

Preparation of the surface on which the leaf is to be laid is crucial. For the best results it should be flawlessly smooth and this is achieved by coating it with gesso. Gesso, pronounced 'jesso', is a creamy substance made by mixing whiting (powdered chalk) with a solution of rabbit-skin glue. Several coats of this are applied and sanded when dry with fine glasspaper. This gesso base is then usually given a coat of red bole. Bole is a red clay pigment (you can get other colours) which when mixed with a little of the glue and painted on to the gesso, gives it a soft velvety finish and provides a good ground colour for the gold leaf.

To make the leaf adhere to this prepared surface it must finally be given a coat of the glue mixed with methylated spirit. The leaf is then laid so that each sheet overlaps the next one. When the glue has 'gone off', excess leaf is lightly brushed off and the rest brought to a high lustre with the burnisher.

The method known as oil gilding usually requires the same gesso base, but the bole is optional. In this technique the gesso or bole surface must be sealed with a coat of shellac. Next a gold size is applied. This is a special mixture of oil varnish and a drying agent. The leaf can only be successfully laid when this size has dried to an appropriate tackiness. Then the leaf is laid on and pressed down with a wad of cotton wool. It cannot be burnished, so it remains matt. Some gold sizes are fast drying and dry in one to two hours. Others take considerably longer. The slower-drying sorts remain at the right tackiness for longer and so are used when large areas are to be gilded.

A much simpler version of oil gilding and one that could be used, say, for regilding slips and small touching-up jobs, is to rub the surface down well with fine wire wool and give it a couple of coats of Venetian red acrylic paint. Rub this down well with wire wool to give a smooth surface. Apply a fast-drying gold size and when tacky lay on some transfer gold.

CHAPTER 9

Old frames

With picture moulding the price it is, re-using and refurbishing second-hand frames becomes a worthwhile proposition. We are not suggesting you start hacking up granny's precious antique frames; in fact if you have an inkling that you're in possession of anything valuable, take it along to a good picture framer for a second opinion before you vandalize it. Antiques apart, and these are best restored by experts, you may have old frames which are still reasonably sound. They may not look exceptional, but with some cleaning and restaining, and perhaps remitred or given a new slip, they can be agreeably transformed and pressed into service for several more years. You have only to look at the price of second-hand frames in some of the junkier 'antique' shops to realize that even the most undistinguished specimens are worth hanging on to.

Basically you have two options if you want to re-use an old wooden frame. If the mitres are still good you can leave it as it is, except for soaking old brown paper off the back and perhaps rubbing the surface down with wire wool, restaining and waxing. You can always use it as a mirror frame – the size in this case is no problem as mirror glass can be cut to fit any frame. Alternatively bend your mind to ways of making the frame suit a new subject. Perhaps cut a fresh mount, and, turning a blind eye to the rule-of-thumb sizes suggested on page **25**, juggle with the border dimensions till you come up with something that *looks* right. If, whatever you do, the subject looks lost or is quite definitely the wrong shape, you might consider finding a second subject that helps to fill the frame (**Fig. 1**). In this case cut a double-windowed mount.

Your second option is to take the frame to bits and remitre the sides. If the corners are already gaping this is usually a simple operation as the frame can be eased apart by waggling

Fig. 1

Fig. 2

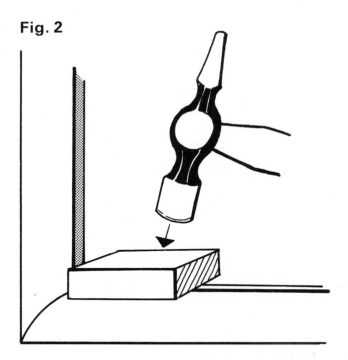

and pulling the corners. When this doesn't work, try clamping the frame in the vice, and, using a piece of wood to protect the moulding, gently knock the frame apart with a hammer **(Fig. 2)**. Sometimes the heads of the nails or pins pull right through the moulding and can then be pulled out with pliers. Other times the heads hold, so the pins are best dislodged by tapping them out with the hammer.

If the corners on a frame are good but you still want to make the frame smaller, you can cut down on your work by just remitring a diagonally opposite pair of corners. In this case separate the frame into two **L** shapes by cutting through a pair of corners (use a hacksaw to negotiate the nails). Then remitre these corners, either cutting off enough to clear the ends of the pins or, if you can only afford to take a little off, using the hacksaw (in the mitre-box guide slots) where necessary to tackle the nails.

Occasionally, having got the frame apart, you'll find the nails have split the wood and perhaps even pulled pieces out. In short the corners are pretty chewed up. It is really not worth cutting off a sliver and attempting to rejoin them in this condition. The corners will be weak and they won't last. Better instead to take a generous amount off and give yourself a fresh section of wood to work on.

Plaster frames, especially the gilded variety, are more awkward to deal with than wooden ones. However, if simple cleaning is all that's required wipe the frame or slip over with white spirit. Small chips in a gilded plaster moulding can be repaired by reshaping with a car body filler. Although sold as car body filler it is recommended for household repairs. This filler can be carved and sanded when dry and then touched up with an appropriate shade of Liquid Leaf. You could use gold or metal leaf (see page **96**), but for minor repairs this would work out rather expensive and fresh leaf rarely matches the tone of a leaf that has aged.

If great chunks of plaster are falling off the moulding it's really a toss-up whether you throw the frame in the dustbin or have it expertly restored at considerable expense. In this situation the intrinsic or sentimental value of the frame is the crucial consideration. A third possibility is to soak the plaster off and lay bare the underlying wooden frame. The frame might be an interesting shape and therefore worth the effort. But the operation can be rather protracted as it involves total immersion of the frame in cold water for about a week or longer. Then of course the wooded frame will need to be scrubbed, sandpapered and finished.

Suppliers

The tools for picture framing can be bought from good tool shops and many DIY shops. Mounting board and fixings are generally available from art shops and picture framers with the possible exception of acid-free board for which a supplier is listed below. Picture mouldings, as mentioned in Chapter 1, can be obtained from some picture framers, otherwise from art shops and DIY stores – look in your Yellow Pages under 'Picture Framers', 'Artists' Materials' or 'Do-it-yourself Shops' and ring to ascertain who stocks what.

Paperchase Products Ltd
213 Tottenham Court Road
London W1
Tel: 01-580 8496
or
167 Fulham Road
London SW3
Tel: 01-589 7873

Exciting variety of papers, including hand-made ones, plus some mount board. Have catalogue and will supply by mail order from Tottenham Court Road branch.

Lawrence & Aitkin Ltd
Albion Works
Kimberley Road
London NW6 7SL
Tel: 01-624 8135

Suppliers of acid-free board and paper.

Buck & Ryan Ltd
101 Tottenham Court Road
London W1
Tel: 01-636 7475

Large tool merchants; have saws, vices, mitre-boxes, etc., plus more sophisticated mitre-cutting equipment. Will supply by mail order.

E. Ploton Ltd
273 Archway Road
London N6
Tel: 01-348 0315

Suppliers of all gilding materials. Have catalogue and will supply by mail order.

Index